S0-BKU-461

THROUGH
PRAYER
TO
REALITY

Douglas A. Rhymes

Vicar of Camberwell, London
and Canon of Southwark Cathedral

Copyright © 1974
by
The Upper Room
1908 Grand Avenue
Nashville, Tennessee 37203

Library of Congress Catalog Card Number: 74-81813

Scripture quotations not otherwise identified are from the King James Version of the Bible.

Scripture quotations identified with the initials RSV are from the Revised Standard Version of the Bible, copyrighted 1946, 1952 and © 1971 by the Division of Christian Education, National Council of the Churches of Christ in the United States of America, and are used by permission.

UR-308-10-0774
Printed in the United States of America

DEDICATION

To John in the peace of whose
home this book was planned
and largely written

CONTENTS

FOREWORD

Douglas A. Rhymes, a distinguished churchman of England, writes that through prayer, and mainly so, one can find the full meaning of life. He stresses the aspect of contemplation and outlines guidance which he has found helpful. In a day when foolish and even bizarre extremes of meditation are being encouraged, it is refreshing to read these balanced and down-to-earth reflections on the art of Christlike contemplation.

Helpfully, he deals with the need to avoid haste and hurry. A sense of timelessness is one of the desired benefits from deep contemplation, and Canon Rhymes speaks eloquently on this subject.

"I play my part by being willing and ready to receive the love of God, by knowing what love means and using that knowledge. . . . Then both prayer and action (or rather the action of reflection and the action of involvement) become filled with the power of God's love poured into my own life."

It is good to taste these words. It will be even better to include them in our way of life.

Wilson O. Weldon
Editor, *The Upper Room*

PREFACE

This book is a sequel to my previous book, *Prayer in the Secular City*. I would still hold firmly to the view of prayer in that book, but I have come to realize in the last few years the increasing importance of the more contemplative side of prayer. Any real understanding of the reality of human life can only come as we search within ourselves to find a deeper knowledge of God and of ourselves as made in his image.

For this reason, in this book I have laid much stress on the contemplative form of praying, and I offer it to all who, in this increasingly meaningless society, are looking for the deep and full realities of human living. Because of this emphasis I have called the book *Through Prayer to Reality*. It is my own hope and prayer that all who read it may find, as I have found, that only through prayer can life have that fullness and abundance of which Christ speaks.

Douglas A. Rhymes

CHAPTER 1
Living and Half-Living

A Sister of a religious community was caught up at Waterloo Station with the crowds of youth returning from the Isle of Wight Pop Festival. The ordinary travelers on the train had quite a rough time from the invasion of the young men and women. Sister, on the other hand, was invited to sit on the platform with them. Propped up against a telephone kiosk, she talked to them about God till one o'clock in the morning. In the end she escaped somewhat weary, but stimulated, to her train. Before she went, she asked one of them, "Why did you fasten on me?" Immediately she received the reply, "You are one of us. You have dropped out." Sister mused as she went on her way—"Perhaps this is what the religious life means: I have dropped out—into God."

Why did these youth select a Sister from a religious community when they would have repudiated with scorn the efforts of any conventional churchgoer to talk to them about God? Their words seemed to indicate that they recognized in her someone who was different—different in that she had chosen to set aside many of the most pressuring values of the world by her choice of the religious vocation and to follow a way of life which is noted for the value it places on both personal and cor-

11

porate prayer. Similarly the young people were reject-
ing, dropping out from the realities of society in which
they lived in search for a greater reality of living, although
perhaps not knowing quite what that reality is. They
were concerned to cut through the hypocrisies and con-
ventions of their day. In their encounter with the Sister,
they were in some sense conscious of one who was in
touch through her faith and prayer with the reality they
were seeking.

Yet it would not be the normal experience of most to
think of prayer as a way of finding reality. This would be
equally true of Christians as of non-Christians. Very few
professing Christians in my experience attach much importance or relevance to prayer, whether it be personal or
that corporate prayer which is commonly called worship.
Many clergy have either given up praying or simply go
through a series of ritual observances like the saying of
Mass or the recitation of morning and evening prayer.
This seems to make little impact on their patterns of
daily living or their motivations of daily action.

Before my present position, I was Director of Lay Training in the Diocese of Southwark, which is mostly South
London. At our training center in Surrey week after week,
I met groups of people from the various parishes to discuss their problems. One of the problems constantly
voiced was the meaninglessness of prayer. It was quite
obvious that for many prayer had become a dead formali-
ty, if engaged in at all. Some of their questions were:
"How can I pray in the way that a man of the twen-
tieth century can with meaning pray?" "How can I make
prayer relevant to my life?" "What am I doing when I
am praying?" They were deeply angry with the clergy
who, they felt, had either simply left them to pray on the
blissful assumption that everyone knew how to do it or
had given them complicated forms and manuals of
prayer. They found these formulas about as useful as a
highly technical book on car maintenance is to a man
who has no mechanical instinct. One young man said,

"Either the clergy are the only people who know how to pray or they dare not say that they do not as this is one of their supposed professional skills." In fact, it became equally clear in moments when they felt free enough to be completely honest, that the clergy did not know how to make prayer a reality to themselves and that many of them had no idea what to do or teach about prayer.

THE UNREALITY OF PRAYER

Before we can think about how we find reality through prayer, we need first to examine what has made prayer unreal in this age. Since life and prayer are intimately connected, if life has lost reality then obviously there will be no reality in prayer. As Coburn says: "The world shapes the spiritual life in the sense that it is the social structures which shape the man. The Church is but one of many social forces and does not have any monopoly upon the control of contemporary spirituality. Therefore the world must be understood if spirituality is to be understood." [1]

But if we suppose that the world has lost its understanding of itself and that the way in which the forces of the world are developing brings less and less reality to the fulfilling of human beings, then a loss of reality in living itself will obviously result in a loss of reality in prayer. This is the tragedy of what is happening: "Most men are only a little alive and to awaken them to a sense of the real in living is a very great responsibility" (T.S. Eliot).

Many writers are seeing the signs of this loss of true living today. Books like Theodore Roszak's *The Making of a Counter Culture* and Charles A. Reich's *The Greening of America* spell it out very clearly:

Of all the forms of impoverishment that can be seen or felt in America, loss of self, or death in life, is surely the most devastating. . . . Beginning with school, if not before, an individual is systematically stripped of his imagination, his creativity, his heritage, his dreams, and his personal uniqueness, in order to style him into a productive unit for a mass technological society. Instinct, feeling, and spontaneity are repressed by overwhelming forces. As the individual is drawn into the meritocracy, his working life is split from his home life and both suffer from a lack of wholeness. Eventually people virtually become their professions, roles, or occupations and are thenceforth strangers to themselves.[2]

If this is what is happening to people, then obviously it is useless to expect that they will be able to step aside from the unreality which has become themselves into that face-to-face reality which is God and which we call prayer. Of course, times of prayer will seem unreal because they *will* be so; they will be an artificial attempt to impose a veneer of reality upon a life which is totally removed from such reality. The veneer will all too quickly wear off because it has no connection with what lies underneath.

This is the basic fallacy of much religious thinking today; it is as pseudo and impoverished as the society in which it exists. One cannot enable a man to live as a law-abiding and socially harmless member of a society in which he has lost his own reality, merely by giving him a dose of individual worship, individual praying, and what is falsely called personal evangelism. This kind of thinking adds as much to his own death and impoverishment as the *Playboy* concept of sexuality adds to the death and impoverishment of true sexuality.

There will be no reality in worship or prayer unless it has been reached through a real rejection of most of what is expected of us by the technological society.

The young—those born after 1940—find themselves living in a society which neither commands nor deserves respect. . . . For has modern man, in his collective existence, laid claim to any god or ideal but the god of possession and enjoyment and the limitless satisfaction of material needs? Has he put forward any reason for working but the reward of pleasure and prosperity? Has he, in fact, evolved anything but this "consumer society" that is so easily and falsely repudiated? [3]

Those who in their religious teachings refuse to disturb the structures of society but concentrate only upon the conversion of the individual do not seem to realize that the reality of the individual as a full person is being stifled by society. Persons will never find the freedom which is theirs as children of God until they have learned through the search of prayer and reflection to make their life a continual protest against the world.

If the structures of society contribute to the unreality of prayer, so does the fact that there is no perspective of living, no philosophy of life in society today, outside the Communist world. Even the Communist philosophy has often been overlaid by the same technocratic and meritocratic poverty of spirit which has characterized the capitalist world. We live in a society which is normally given two names—secular and permissive. Neither of these words constitutes a view of living which could rightly be called a philosophy. The word *secular* simply means "this present age," so a secular society is simply the society in which we happen to live today. The word *permissive* simply means a society which "permits," that is, which allows an individual to decide for himself his way of living.

The opposite of a permissive society is an authoritarian society in which the individual is ordered to live in a certain way. Insofar as a permissive society treats people as adults while an authoritarian society treats them as children, it is obviously to be preferred. But the present-day society is basically a neutral and indifferentist society, a society in which it does not matter what you believe so long as you believe it doesn't matter, as Chesterton described it. It has no concern with ultimate reality, meaning and purpose in living, or truth as an experience of the real, but is simply a society which tolerates many opinions and which gives no divine right to any of them.

The church is simply one minority among many minorities, and belief in God is simply a minority opinion held by an increasingly small number of people. Ours is a society characterized by a materialistic, functional spirit in which the main questions asked are "Does it work?" or "Is it relevant?" We live in an age of rapid change in which an old age is dying and a new age is painfully being born, but no one really knows what this new age is striving for or trying to be. Life is characterized by a shaking of the foundations of religious faith, of a shattering of the old images which satisfied our ancestors but which do not satisfy us. Religious faith is dead for many people and the word *God* has no meaning. For a short period even certain theologians produced a "death of God" theology which as a theology had as short a life as it deserved, but the death of God has certainly become a fact of life for some people.

As for the so-called permissive society, it is basically very nonpermissive. Conformity has grown rather than diminished; the pressures of advertisement have molded us into the "units which pass through the entrails of a computer" with which the manipulators of a consumer society can most easily deal. Minorities which do not conform, be they racial or sexual (e.g., immigrants within another culture or homosexuals in a heterosexual society), are only very grudgingly tolerated.

In fact, permissiveness in the thought of most people has come to mean a permissiveness of sexuality which is increasingly divorced from personal relationship—an exploration of the techniques through which orgasm may be experienced rather than a matter of binding loyalties and personal attachments. "The perfect playboy practices a career enveloped by noncommittal trivialities: there is no home, no family, no romance that divides the heart painfully. Life off the job exhausts itself in a constant run of imbecile affluence and impersonal orgasms." [4] The woman in the permissive society has become the "bunny-girl," the mindless decoration, the playmate of man. Sex has increasingly become not a reality of the unity of the physical with the mental and spiritual— the wholeness of persons—but rather a series of technical experiments to make the release of the sperm less boring.

The result then of both the secular and the permissive society has been to produce an age in which there is no meaning, no faith, no purpose or goal of living, no depth of relationship; everything is functional and dispensable. Such a climate is obviously deterrent to any concept of prayer since prayer is concerned with meaning, with faith, with purpose, with relationship.

I would not wish there to be misunderstanding here. Society's demand for functional use is a very right demand; we must ask the question of prayer as of all other aspects of living, "Does it work?" As I said in my last book, we should heed the empirical and pragmatic demands of modern man in a spirituality which is seen to work and to relate to a deeper understanding of this world rather than some other world. The irony is that the very way in which the secular society has evolved prevents it from functioning properly, for proper functioning demands a clear concept of what is real, what is purpose, what is goal. No society can continue without faith in what it stands for and what it is setting out to achieve. It is the very lack of that within present-day society which is causing so much discontent and so much searching for new ways of living and thinking. I shall endeavor to show throughout this book that it is through prayer that reality is found and that this is, indeed, the very heart and function of prayer.

Prayer may then seem to many to be irrelevant to present-day society, but, in fact, it is the way through which society and persons within society find a form of living that is not half-living but true living. It is the fault of both society and of the way in which our churches have taught it that prayer has been thought irrelevant. Society failed in not realizing that without a philosophy of life, without a sense of meaning and goal, functionalism will degenerate into a death-giving conformism. The fault of the churches is found in teaching that prayer is something you do as an extra to living rather than as the search for the meaning of life itself.

As one young man expressed it at one of our conferences, "We have been taught to *say* our prayers rather than to *pray* our lives." Bishop Robinson puts it this way, "Prayer is conceived in terms of turning aside from the business of 'the world' to 'be with God.' However much the various methods and techniques of prayer may differ, they all tend to start from the assumption that prayer is to be *defined* in terms of what one does in the times of *dis*engagement." [5] Perhaps, however, it would have been better had he said that the fault of the teaching on prayer is that prayer has been conceived as separate from living. Disengagement is rightly a part of living. Unless we are obsessed with the Protestant ethic about the virtue of work, we know that our times of contemplative reflection are as truly activity as our times of going about the world's business. Quiet, withdrawal, solitude are just as essential for health as involvement, participation, and engagement. Real life is as much found within oneself as it is in involvement with others.

Prayer then is the means by which in both engagement and disengagement we search for reality. It is not a saying of prayers in ten minutes apart from life, nor is it a living for others with no time for reflection; prayer is neither pietism nor activism.

THE SEARCH FOR MEANING

It is one of those paradoxes of life that the very nature of our technocratic and secularistic society which has made prayer so difficult and meaningless to many has also helped to create a new search for meaning. This is bringing many back to prayer as properly understood and taught by the great spiritual leaders of the past. Within this materialistic civilization there is a vast discontent, a longing to find a meaning to life. The whole book *The Greening of America* is the story of this new consciousness of living which seeks totally to reverse the values of the technocratic society.

We find this search in many different quarters and many different ways: the sense of restlessness among young people and their search for communities in which life and people can again have worth and significance; the return to the stage of the figure of Christ, as a symbol of joy and freedom; the questions raised by many novelists and dramatists are questions of "Who am I?" "What is true living and how is it found?"; the interest in the meaning of God as indicated by the questions of the returning youth from the pop festival and by my own experience in talking to students; the seeking after holiness and contemplative prayer found in the great crowds who flock to hear Archbishop Anthony Bloom and in the large numbers who attend lectures and training in the contemplative prayer of the East given by gurus; the increased attendance at retreats; the horror at the realization that sin is no longer even great sin but meaningless violence and cowardly assaults on the old and defenseless (of this the situation in Northern Ireland is typical—no heroic rebellion, no assassinations of political enemies, but simply stupid and cruel attacks upon ordinary people). All these facts have awakened many to the realization that a world without meaning is a world increasingly barren, dehumanizing, and rottenly vicious without worth, dignity, or purpose.

So the stage is set for that search for reality, which is unconditional and vulnerable, that living the *now* of our daily life with an understanding of its why and where. This is what is meant by a praying of life. That search for reality in all its forms will now occupy us for the rest of book.

CHAPTER 2

Praying My Life

If I am to find reality through prayer, how do I begin? For me, the search focuses on four personal needs—the need to experience, observe, and evaluate life; the need to reflect upon and explore at a deeper level the life which I am experiencing; the need to know myself and to be able to respond to my personal needs and the needs of others to whom I am related in life; and the need to know God—the ultimate reality behind all life. Let us consider each one of these in greater detail.

The need to experience, observe, and evaluate life: For most of us, prayer will start not from the ultimate question of who God is but from the more immediate question of where and who am I. The advice which Jesus gave to his disciples was, "Watch and pray" (Mark 14:38, RSV). For us as well, watching is the necessary preliminary to praying. Only those who are watching carefully will be able to see what God is doing in his world now, make the necessary connections between events and causes, find the work to which we are called, and understand our personal experiences of pain and joy.

Prayer must be rooted in what is happening in the world around me. Prayer is trying to understand what is happening and being willing to get involved in what is happening. Of course, I can be the sort of person who simply allows life to go on around me, impinging upon me only when it affects my own comfort or happiness. For example, I shall be interested in the high cost of living only because it affects my own pocket; I shall know the difficulties of housing only when I cannot get good living conditions; I shall know what love means only when I go through the ephemeral experience of "falling in love." Unfortunately if I am that sort of person, I can never know what prayer means. I may occasionally put up the kind of "gimme" prayer—"Gimme this, gimme that, or don't gimme this or that," but I am revealing by such so-called praying that I have never grown up.

To be the kind of person who knows what prayer is, I need to observe carefully what is happening around me. It takes effort to understand the economic circumstances which lie behind inflation or the difficulties which prevent adequate housing. I must learn from my knowledge of the joys, the pains, and the problems of life around me that much more is demanded of me than the emotional response to a "falling-in-love situation." I need, therefore, to be the kind of person who not only experiences life but is accustomed to observing and evaluating the experience. I cannot, in living, make valid decisions of power, of morality, of human relationship, unless I have been in the fullest sense a watcher of life.

The need to explore at a deeper level my experiences: But if I am to pray my life, I must go beyond the ordinary observations upon living, however careful and accurate they are. My primary concern lies with what these experiences reveal of the deeper levels of living. When we begin to become conscious of the differences between good and evil, between heaven and hell, between the kingdom of God and the kingdom of this world, then we are exploring at a deeper level the world in which we are placed. We are beginning to understand why many are protesting against the impersonality and inhumanity of life today, what is the aching void at the center of our hysterical restlessness, the emptiness which lies behind much of our activity. A psychiatrist observed in a group which was discussing prayer that "true prayer was not something with which believers cushioned themselves against the stark realities of life, but that it was the quest for the purpose of life, for the individual's place in that purpose, and for authentic relationships with others, in which there was giving as well as receiving."

This awareness of the world around us at its deeper level is most completely illustrated in the prophetic writings of the Bible. First, the prophet has a penetrating observation as a result of his experience, but then sees what is happening in the deeper terms of "thus saith the Lord." Like all other activities of the spiritual life, it is an awareness discovered only when love is prepared to take time to see beneath the situation to the Word of God upon the situation. "Prayer could be silent, a way of being in the world, an inward and outward bearing, a constant striving for increased awareness of the world, and for the active love, ever renewed, which must accompany this striving." These words of Petru Dumitriu in his novel *Incognito* sum up the kind of reaching out to the reality behind and beneath experience which is what matters in the praying life.

The need to know myself and to be able to respond to myself and to others: Teilhard de Chardin in *The Phenomenon of Man* writes: "Reflection is . . . the power acquired by a consciousness to turn in upon itself, to take possession of itself *as of an object* endowed with its own particular consistence and value: no longer merely to know, but to know oneself; no longer merely to know, but to know that one knows." [1] But what does it mean to know myself? If we know the answer to that, we know why that knowledge can only be reached through prayer. The answer truly is very simple. My real self is that I am made in the image of God. My real self is the potential divinity within me which it is the purpose of my life to bring to fulfillment: "You, therefore, must be perfect, as your heavenly Father is perfect" (Matthew 5:48, RSV).

The connection between myself and the nature of God is made almost shockingly clear by the great mystics of the past: "Our created being abides in the Eternal Essence, and is one with it in its essential existence" (Ruysbroeck). Another goes even further: "The essential meaning of religion is not to know God as one knows a friend; it is to *become* God, for to know Him is to take Him into our inmost self as the fulfillment of that self; and it is only in *becoming* Him that we know Him." St. Athanasius affirms this in simple terms lest one should think that what has been said is arrogant heresy: "God was made man in order that man might be made God." So then on the highest authority, the true me is the God in me, the God whom I hope in terms of ultimate fulfillment to become.

If then I think of God as both the ground of my own being and the ultimate reality behind all life, it follows that the more I truly know and work to become myself, the more I am in union with God. The essence of prayer is union with God. Through prayer I shall become more conscious of my true self, live more in accord with the nature of my true being, participate more in the divine nature. This knowledge of myself is also the way by which I learn to live what St. Paul calls "the life of Christ in me." In this new life, the pseudo-nature is replaced by my true nature at a higher level of consciousness. The standard of measurement by which I may judge when this divine self in me is being fulfilled is always the standard of the divine humanity which is Jesus Christ—"attain . . . to mature manhood, to the measure of the stature of the fulness of Christ" (Ephesians 4:13, RSV).

With this understanding, prayer becomes the way in which I can penetrate through the conscious to the unconscious or subconscious (using terms of modern psychology). Why? Because if God is the ground of my being, then insofar as I enter deeply into communion with God, I am also reaching the deepest levels of my own being— the self which lies beneath my more superficial and conscious self. I think this explains the keen interest among young people in Eastern forms of prayer and in the knowledge gained through certain forms of drugs, namely LSD. Both are seen as means by which one penetrates through the conscious to the unconscious self. The difference is that taking drugs will, in fact, never lead us to the knowledge of our true selves, for it is a shortcut to knowledge, gained by artificial means. Drugs actuallv produce their own toll of disintegration betweeen the conscious and the unconscious self. The result is not one of integration between the real me and the phenomenal me but a division of almost a Jekyll-and-Hyde nature.

On the other hand, the interest in Eastern forms of prayer may be the result of the great insight of Hinduism that the ego or the self of which one is conscious is not the true self at all. In Indian philosophy this external self disappears when the body dies, to be replaced by that true immortal self, the divine spark within us which is of the same essence as God himself. The Hindu formula of faith is basically "Thou art That." The sad thing is that in the great Christian mystics of the past, like Paul, Saint John of the Cross, John Ruysbroeck, Saint Teresa, Richard Rolle de Hampole, there is exactly the same teaching of the way through prayer to the divine self in me. Unfortunately we have lost that tradition in our Christian teaching. The recovery of the true Christian contemplative prayer might wel! win back many to the Christian church.

The knowledge of my true self better enables me to respond to my personal needs and the needs of others. Through prayer, I find the way to that abundant life of which Christ speaks and which in me he has come to bring. I find the gifts for which all people are striving— the love which transcends loneliness, the freedom which is true and lasting, the humility which enables me to deal with what the world calls success.

Through union with God in prayer, the limits of confined humanity are breached. My loneliness is assuaged not by a mere quantity of experiences, activities, and relationships but by the gift of God within me. I am anchored in that within me which is a union of security, love, consistency, and eternity. I cannot be alone because my roots are in God, and he is forever in my heart and in my whole being in a way that no human being can ever be. He is in me and I in him in complete union.

Perhaps if we could view Holy Communion in this way, it would be no longer dull and irrelevant but as vital and exciting as a date with someone we love. Recently I was talking with a lady in my parish who said that she found the only real bond of union between herself and the fellow-members of her church lay in their common roots in Communion. This was a bond which existed nowhere else outside the church, for here she found those with whom she could talk, find release, the mitigation of loneliness. The experience had such depth and meaning for her because the union lay in the same roots —the bread, broken in love and glorified by the presence of the common ground of all their beings.

Union with God also brings a new sense of freedom because the only ultimate freedom is that which cannot be subjected to pressures. My limited external humanity will always be subjected to the pressures of status, success, fear, power, and greed. Even when people heroically strive for freedom from some form of tyranny, there is always the danger that the freedom they achieve will itself become another form of tyranny. Communism brings freedom from the slavery of capitalist competition but can become a form of state domination; Black Power brings freedom from white domination but can easily replace it with black domination; freedom from parental pressures by the young may easily be replaced with slavery to peer-group pressures. True freedom has its ground in God, not in the world, because only in God is there a lack of causal determination. God is spirit, and spirit is not subject to causal pressures. Therefore persons are only free when they are enabled to transcend their ordinary limited humanity and to center their being in that which cannot be enslaved.

We find this kind of freedom in Christ and in the great saints. "They reveal to other men what man can be; they smash the body to atoms and come forth a living flame with a body newly refreshed; they unearth the hidden beauty in human beings. . . . But, above all, the saints possess some secret of peace, as if, like the successful lover, they were in possession of their heart's desire." [2] That secret of peace is the perfect freedom spoken of by St. Paul in describing the union with Christ, with the God in me. Prayer then is the means by which I may patiently and persistently convert my whole life into the freedom of that peace and love. Freedom is given out of God's love, enabling my true self to surface into the world.

Likewise, I find the humility to deal with what the world calls success as I am united with God. Simone Weil puts this well: "It is only from the light which streams constantly from heaven that a tree can derive the energy to strike its roots deep into the soil. The tree is, in fact, rooted in the sky." [3] So persons are rooted in God and find all that they can be in fulfillment and growth through God.

It may seem that if a person is rooted in the world, his success will be what he can achieve through the use of the material structure of the world, but this is not so. The only true success I can ever know in life is that which is given me through the realization of the divine spark within me. My hungers, my desires, my fears, my hopes, my dreams, and my actions all turn beyond the successes of the world. My true reality, my true success is revealed in the ancient phrase: *Teneo quid teneor* ("I hold that in which I am held"). I know that without this union with God I shall never know success in life, and yet this success is in no way due to me or controlled by me.

John Ruysbroeck puts it thus:

> This essential union of our spirit with God does not exist in itself, but it dwells in God, and it flows forth from God . . . and it returns to God as to its Eternal Origin. And in this wise it has never been, nor ever shall be, separated from God; for this union is within us by our naked nature, and, were this nature to be separated from God, it would fall into pure nothingness.

In other words, the success I achieve in life is simply due to the knowledge of my true self as the Christ within me, the divine humanity within me, and what I do is simply the result of this union. I shall know that my deeds, however good, are not the result of the efforts of my conscious self but the deeds which spring only from my roots in God.

The need to know God: I have spent a good deal of time writing of the need to know myself because it is through this primary knowledge of myself that I come to know God. If my true self is the divine self in me, then obviously this leads to a deeper knowledge of God. In view, however, of the endless debates of the last few years on what we mean by *God,* we should spend a little time on the consideration of this question.

It must be said immediately that I cannot know God simply through the mind. This is, perhaps, one of the greatest difficulties today because of the excessive premium put on scientific knowledge requiring proof and facts. Our world is crowded with facts; our passion is to discover facts, to prove everything. We have developed what might be called a "lust for knowledge." Facts and proof for the sake of facts and proof have become for many the same thing as truth, and this is not so.

Within this view of the world there can be very little

knowledge of God. If the only kind of knowledge we will accept is the knowledge based upon touch, sight, and reason, then it is very difficult, if not impossible, to know God. There is no visual image we can make of God. If we try to do so, we shall be led straight into the kind of anthropomorphism which has so bedeviled the Christian faith and which Bishop Robinson spent so much time in rightly dismissing as the "God out there." Furthermore, there are no words with which we can adequately describe God, because by the very nature of the word *God* we are speaking of that which is beyond human experience and thus beyond language. By intellectual or scientific proofs, I can neither prove nor, for that matter, disprove the existence of God. It is useless to deal with the knowledge of God on that kind of level.

But there are many other levels of knowledge besides the intellectual. For example, knowledge is revealed by the poet and by the artist. An artist is making a statement about reality in a very different way from a scientist, but it is equally a statement about reality. The kind of truth that art communicates is not a factual or verifiable truth but a truth found in images which communicate meaning and which evoke responses of the emotions. It is perhaps significant that in the course of Christian history something of the transcendence, beauty, and love of God has been better communicated through the paintings of Michelangelo, the glory of ancient cathedrals, and the writing of great poets, than through creeds and philosophies. Even today many people catch something of a reality not found in the secularist world when they visit Ely Cathedral or gaze upon the roof of the Sistine Chapel.

Even the artist does not really succeed, however, in enabling us to find our knowledge of God. Our knowledge of God is found only through union with him in prayer and living. This can be dimly understood in comparison to the union with another human being which we call love. When we say that we know someone we love, we are describing a kind of knowledge not obtained either through science or through art. We know people by being with them, by a kind of union with them in life. The more we merge into each other, that is, are united with each other, the deeper the knowledge becomes and yet the more difficult it is to describe. When two people truly love each other, they find it almost impossible to describe that love, yet no one can shake them from the knowledge of its reality. The knowledge of God is like this.

The great psychologist Jung puts it like this: "Every day I am thankful to God that I have been allowed to experience the reality of the divine image within me. Had this not been granted to me I should indeed have been a bitter enemy of Christianity. But thanks to this act of grace my life has meaning and my inward eye has been opened to the beauty and greatness of dogma. On the strength of my psychological experience I consider dogma to be an immense psychological truth which I need not *believe* since I *know* it." In other words, it is not in the intellectual formulation of the dogma that Jung finds his belief in God, but he welcomes these formulations because he has already found through union with God that he knows him personally. The formulations simply put into words a knowledge which has not come through the mind but through that love expressed in union with God.

We say as a dogma to describe God, "God is love." But this dogma becomes real only insofar as we know what love means and what therefore we mean when we say that we love. In other words, when we know how to love, we shall know God. Nowhere is this more beautifully expressed than when Dame Julian of Norwich summed up a series of visions which she had received in these words: "Wouldst thou learn thy Lord's meaning in this thing? Learn it well: Love was His meaning. Who shewed it thee? Love. What shewed He thee? Love. Wherefore shewed it He? For Love." Or again in the words of First John: "If we love one another, God dwelleth in us, and his love is perfected in us" (1 John 4:12).

What does this word *love* mean? To many it is a feeling or an emotion, but it would be absurd to say that God is feeling or emotion, even multiplied by the infinite. Love is obviously not just feeling. To many love is sexual attraction, but to say "God is sexual attraction" is even more absurd. To many love is possessive and devouring, but God is not possessive or devouring—rather is he liberating and fulfilling. One very striking and helpful explanation of love is found in Soloviev's *Meaning of Love*. His thesis is that man is a creature of absolute significance and worth and the sole reason of his existence is that he may attain to perfection through union with God. Man does not, however, remain isolated in his own uniqueness. Love comes to him and makes him aware of the equal significance and worth of another human being and fills him with the desire to give himself to this other, to be united with him or her, and enable the other to realize their own potentiality of perfection. This means to see the image of God in the other person and to love him or her for God's sake and in God. Therefore in human love, what happens first is feeling and emotion, but when the feeling is translated into a deep sense of union, security, and action, true love enters in.

If to love means to live in the beloved more than in oneself, then it means that the lover enters into and shares the desires and will of the other, seeking to fulfill them rather than his own. In other words it is when the enjoyment of a feeling has been succeeded by the working at (often at some cost) a relationship that human love comes to resemble the love which is of God.

To understand this is to understand what is meant by love and therefore what is meant by knowing God. God is unknowable by the mind; we do not reach God by thinking about him. But God can be known in a depth relationship with him, and this relationship finds expression through the praying of life. When I start from the sense of my own significance and worth and reach out to the significance and worth of God, when I desire more than anything else to give myself to God, when I want the union between myself and God to be the means of fulfilling myself, then I begin to know God.

I have written at some length what the search for reality through prayer will involve. My concern now is to move on to the specific details of this kind of prayer pilgrimage. The first step I wish to describe is the deep reflection upon living, myself, and God which is called contemplative prayer. Following that and equally important is the illumination of life which comes from praying with the Bible. These are the necessary preliminaries to the Prayer of the Now of life, the learning to pray one's life in the actual processes and situations of life itself. In the final part of the book I will be considering the Prayer of Togetherness (the prayer of the group or communal worship) and the Prayer of Finality (the prayer of the end of life and facing death).

CHAPTER 3

The Prayer of Reflection

In my last book *Prayer in the Secular City,* I said, "If there is to be this kind of understanding of life (i.e., 'the glory of God is man fully alive') there must be the opportunity of standing back from life . . . that we may learn to understand reality and bear truth." I would wish not only to say this again but to emphasize it even more than I did then.

In the years that have passed since 1967, the search for reality of living has been clearly seen in the agonizing and frustrated search of many young people. That search has led to all kinds of undesirable shortcuts like drugs, black magic, profit-making, and phony gurus. I believe that Christian contemplation can answer this search. It demands from those who start on the journey nothing less than a total response—a costly experience making us vulnerable and open to God, ourselves, and others. In other words, contemplative prayer, far from being an escape from action and the praying of life, becomes an inescapable preliminary to any understanding of what life means.

Even those who are not necessarily Christians know the need, if living is to be true, of standing back, reflecting, becoming temporarily dis-involved. The humanist writer Albert Camus says that to understand the world, it is necessary sometimes to turn away from the world; to serve men better, it is necessary for a moment to keep them at a distance.

One of the early difficulties in the practice of contemplation is the feeling of guilt when we are not being what the world calls "active." Society, especially Protestant society, has made such a virtue of work that activity is considered to be virtuous and passivity wicked. This has affected even the lives of the clergy who feel quite ashamed to be "caught" in their studies simply reading or thinking and feel the need to apologize. One of my churchwardens on looking through the window and finding me reading said with some acerbity, "How nice to have nothing to do but read."

THE OBSESSION WITH ACTIVITY

It is important that we should know how to deal with this obsession with activity—one of the most insidious pressures of modern life. Let us face it for the absurdity that it is. First, it presupposes that we are working only when we are rushing frantically about doing one job after another, arriving at one committee late and leaving early to arrive late at the next, placing ourselves endlessly at the disposal of other people's "needs" (which is often only another way of showing how much we ourselves need to be needed). It is equally work when we are learning to be still, when we are learning in the quiet of reflection to look hard at the world, at ourselves, and, above all, at God, and when we are refreshing our minds and stimulating our thoughts through the reading of other people's ideas. It may well be that this is the kind of work that our overpressurized and overactive world needs more badly than any other.

In the second place, if we place such a premium on activity, we shall increasingly make those who are unable to be active—the retired, the old, the disabled—feel inadequate and unwanted. This is quite important in an age when many people reach the peak of their business and professional attainment at quite an early age and when retirement is often many years before death. If there has been no place in their life for quiet, reflection, and reading, older persons are going to find the latter years of life a desert of boredom, frustration, and depression. In fact, our psychiatric hospitals are becoming increasingly full of older people who are depressed for this reason.

If we are overactive, we very easily have the feeling that we are indispensable, and this is human pride at its worst. It comes as quite a shock during a time of illness (often a kindly way of dealing with overactivity) to realize that even without us life goes along quite steadily and without crisis. Then, when the shock has subsided, we can rest peacefully and without guilt in the knowledge that we are not the centers of our world. We are learning through our dispensability the valuable lesson of humility.

Most important of all is the realization that activity itself is only valuable and worthwhile if its goals and purpose have been carefully estimated and evaluated beforehand. The more important the activity in life, whether it be in work, social planning, or personal relationships, the more we shall need to look hard at our motivation, the reality of what we are doing, and the possible implications and consequences of action. Christ was well aware of this. Before every important occasion of his life, he went away to be quiet and to think. The beginning of his ministry literally drove him into the wilderness to wrestle with what could have been ruinous activities in his ministry. For example, the choice of his disciples necessitated a whole night of thorough and careful evaluation. The need to meet pain, loneliness, dereliction, and death led him into the peace and stillness of Gethsemane. He also felt no guilt about taking time off; however much people needed him, he sometimes withdrew from them when he knew that he could not meet their needs without the withdrawal.

THE WAY OF CONTEMPLATION

To avoid confusion, I need to say that I am not dealing with contemplative prayer in a purely technical sense. In all books on mystical theology, there is a distinction made between various types of reflective praying. There is *vocal prayer;* namely, prayer by means of words—intercession, confession, petition, and thanksgiving. This is so often the only kind of prayer which many Christians have ever been taught; and yet for many it is the most useless form of prayer, for it is neither reflection upon life nor the living out of life. It has a place, but for many it is a dead and barren labor separated from living rather than deeply connected with it. The way by which such articulation can be connected with living I shall hope to show later in this book. There is *meditation* in which themes are presented, thought out, and resolutions made. When we come to think of praying with the Bible, we shall have in mind something of what is often called meditation on this level. But meditation will often pass over into contemplation when seeing, intuition, and reflection combine. Then there is *affective* prayer in which acts of affection, aspiration, and hope play an important part. Finally there is *contemplative prayer* in which spiritual intuition and simple seeing replace all words and intellectual thinking.

In view of these technical divisions, I am thinking of contemplative prayer as being all those times of living when one is practicing recollection, concentration, and the capacity of intuitive looking into the reality of all life. The latter will be a gift from God which will come to us as we prepare ourselves to receive it. The aim and motivation of ordinary living are not divided from those periods when we stand aside from life in order that we may live it more fully and with greater reality. For the Christian, the end of man is union with God in love, and we are meant to know something of that union both through contemplation and involvement (loving relationship with one another in God). There is no either/or —both are necessary.

I can best describe contemplative prayer by outlining some of its basic requirements.

First, it involves a search for that knowledge of myself which can come to me when I am not supported by the "props" of life—the many activities in which I am engaged, the people who are surrounding me with the various roles which they put upon me. Therefore I shall be seeking knowledge which can only truly come to me when I am alone and still before God. St. Francis said, "Man is man only as he is alone before God." Solitude and stillness are necessary to the search for reality in myself. "What we are worth when motionless, is the question. There is a density of being in a Dominican at prayer. He is never so much alive as when prostrate and motionless before his God. In Pasteur, holding his breath over the microscope, there is a density of being. . . . Cézanne, mute and motionless before his sketch, is an inestimable presence. He is never more alive than when silent, when feeling and pondering." [1]

Contemplative prayer also requires training to be the kind of person who is willing to take time in order that things, myself, and God may be known. Perhaps one of the gravest indictments of our civilization is that we think it almost sinful to stand and stare; everything is a rush against time. Michel Quoist, in a very fine poem about time, writes that we are always fighting against time when, in fact, we have all the time of eternity. Even our worship of God has to be within the hour; the sermon is judged not by its quality but by its brevity. The newspaper which is popular is the tabloid which takes little time to read.

We would fail altogether to understand today the lovely story of the old peasant who spent hours before the altar and when asked why, replied, "I just looks at him and he looks at me." I can readily recall an incident one day outside St. Giles Centre (a Samaritan center associated with our parish). In the courtyard facing the busy street sat a young man cross-legged in prayer, absolutely still for over two hours. It almost stopped the life of Camberwell, for people crowded round to watch, the buses stopped, and the police asked if he should be moved on. Truly did Oscar Wilde say, "While in the opinion of the world contemplation is the gravest sin of which any citizen can be guilty, in the opinion of the highest culture it is the proper occupation of man."

I remember on a visit to New York standing in the middle of that city and wondering if the people there ever gave themselves time to think and to wonder, and whether the city would be the hell of crime and fear that it is if the prayers of the inhabitants were not probably as thin as the haste with which they live their outer lives. It is sometimes a great relief and joy to go to worship in an Orthodox church where there is still a sense of timelessness.

The contemplative person takes time perceiving and evaluating reality, believing that it takes time to know anything or anyone, and still more time to know oneself and to know God. But the time we give is not just a time of observation, but rather the time to know by a process of absorption—seeing things from the inside rather than from the outside. Of the two ways of approaching reality, F. C. Happold writes,

> One view is that it is an intelligible presentation which is spread out before us for our detached and dispassionate examination; its nature to be grasped by thought, analysis, and classification. . . . Another view is that the world is not like that at all, that it is a mystery. . . . To penetrate its deepest secrets one must . . . try to feel it, to become part of it. One must be content, intently and humbly, to "contemplate" it, to gaze at it as one gazes at a picture, not in order to analyze the technique of its brushwork or color arrangement, but to penetrate its meaning and significance.[2]

We sometimes talk of getting inside something or someone in order to understand it or him. By so doing, what we are seeking to understand becomes part of us. It is that process which absorbs the time of contemplation. To quote Happold again, it is a "self-forgetting attention, a humble receptiveness, a still and steady gazing, an intense concentration, so that emotion, will, and thought are all fused and then lost in something which is none of them, but which embraces them all." [3]

Another requirement of contemplation is the realization of what learning the love of God is likely to mean in terms of prayer. We are so accustomed to thinking of love as a beautiful emotional experience that we expect our time of communion with God to be all sweetness, glow, and comfort. Sometimes at first, this is the case but little by little we learn that experiencing the love of God is much more like the experience of the love of someone to whom you are married. With that person you are learning the costly business of what it is like to live with another human being rather than the ephemeral experience of falling in love. Sometimes we shall be utterly bored with God; sometimes we shall find his demands intolerable; sometimes we shall want to escape from him; frequently we shall find it more than difficult, quite crucifying in fact to live with him; sometimes we shall be furiously angry with him. Unless we learn to be free to express all this in our prayer, we shall not know what it is to love him.

What is happening in our time of prayer is that we are learning in relation to God what we are regularly learning in all human relationships. In both cases our love and desire are being tested to their foundations. Perhaps we would find this easier if we did not live in this pseudo-permissive society which has failed to realize that love is not merely an emotional and sexual attraction, but a somewhat painful working at the art of learning to live with and understand another human being.

Even though we might argue that the end of man is union with God, that union is not without pain. St. Bernard said that man is the cross upon which Christ is stretched. If we, therefore, are to know the divine in us

which is God, we must expect that it will be known only
through the emptying of that which is ordinary man. It
is difficult to put into practice the old adage "Empty
yourself and know that I am God." But if we are truly
empty and then offer all that we are to wait upon God
in the desire of love, we shall grow in the way of naked
faith, hope, and love which is *not* dependent upon conscious realization of pleasure or emotional experience.
And because, as in all relationships, there is the infusion
of love from God's side so that it is not just I who am
willing to live with God but God who is willing to live
with me, then growth in the knowledge and love of
God helps to unify life. Contemplation and action are together. I play my part by being willing and ready to receive the love of God, by knowing what love means, and
by using that knowledge in life and in reflection upon
life. Then both prayer and action (or rather the action of
reflection and the action of involvement) become filled
with the power of God's love poured into my own life.

THE BACKGROUND OF CONTEMPLATIVE PRAYER

The whole teaching of the Bible and of all the great
spiritual leaders of the past points to the necessity for
external and internal silence, in order to reflect deeply on
the reality of life and God. The psalmist says, "Wait on
the Lord" (Psalm 27:14). Our Lord counsels: "When you
pray, go into your room and shut the door and pray to
your Father who is in secret" (Matthew 6:6, RSV). Yet this
teaching would seem to conflict with some people's experience of life today because we are so accustomed to
noise. Many younger people find it necessary to have
noise in order to concentrate. If you go into a youth club,
you will often find that it is not only necessary to have
noise but very loud noise at that. If noise is acceptable,
then silence becomes unbearable.

I spoke in my last book of the young man who did a
complicated Ph.D. dissertation to a background of pop
music. Silence is an increasingly uncommon quality in

life. We are constantly assailed by outward noise—the increase of traffic on the road, the automatic turning on of the radio or television as soon as we enter the house, background music in stores, hotels, factories, and railway stations. Should we then drop the idea that silence is necessary to deep reflection? At one time I thought this might be so, but I have changed my view because it has become clear to me that the basic reason for the noise is to *stop* people from thinking. We have so lost the art of communication that we use the noise to save us the trouble of communicating. Loud discothèque music makes conversation impossible—and for many, this is a great relief since there is nothing to talk about anyway. The same is equally true of radios, records, and television. The family does not know what to say to each other, so they save themselves the trouble.

Granted, some have become so accustomed that they can only concentrate with background noise of some kind, this is like saying that some alcoholics can only act normally when they have had a drink, that many drug addicts cannot attain any degree of clarity in thought or action until they have had their "fix." If noise has become an addiction, then we should try to cure people of the addiction, rather than assuming that the addiction must continue. I still believe that the need for silence as in the experiences of Moses, Elijah, Christ, Paul, and the great mystics is a valid one for any who are trying to find deeper reality through prayer.

The real difficulty for all of us is not to stop exterior noise but to find interior stillness. Everywhere the interior is being penetrated as well as the exterior. Wherever we go, even within our own homes, advertisements are screaming at us—the hidden persuaders of mankind. Television brings into our homes the horror of the sin and anguish of mankind in a way that the spoken or written word could never do. High-rise flats with their limited space for children reduce many a woman to nervous tension. The anxieties and pressures of the rat race cause many men and women to bring back into their homes the interior pressures of their work so that relaxation even after work becomes very difficult. The fears of modern life are driving persons into various forms of mental stress, and mental illness is increasing. No wonder the state of turmoil in which we live makes interior silence ever more difficult.

Yet the very nature of the increase of stress makes it even more necessary to find stillness and interior peace. Because of this, it is not surprising that there is more demand for retreats, that many of the words of our pop songs speak of stillness within (I think particularly of the folk songs of Leonard Cohen or Joan Baez), and that the ways of Yoga and the Eastern contemplatives are being sought after by the younger generation. The very world we live in produces a demand which will be met, either by the Christian church or elsewhere. In the next chapter I shall try to give various techniques by which we may learn to practice the art of silence and stillness.

Another interesting facet of contemplation relates to the use of the body. One of the most important results of the influences of Eastern mysticism, especially Yoga, is that we in the Western world have at last begun to pay attention to the effect the body has upon our capacity for concentration and reflection. We should have always known this. As long ago as the writing of the book of the Wisdom of Solomon, the author remarks: "For a perishable body weighs down the soul, and this earthly tent burdens the thoughtful mind" (Wisdom 9:15, RSV). Of course, we have long been aware that a tired body, a painful body, a flabby body will have its effect upon our powers of concentration, but it is only recently that it has become recognized that there are ways of posture, ways of breathing, ways of exercise which can help to promote the redemption of the body and make it one with the mind and the spirit in the search for reality.

Training in the use of the body in prayer and worship has been almost entirely neglected. We generally assume that we stand to sing and kneel to pray and sit to listen, but no one has bothered to tell us how to stand, how to sit, how to kneel. Until recently we did not think of the dance or the gestures of bodily affection such as a kiss or a handshake as having anything to do with prayer or worship. Now, however, through the teaching of such people as Father Slade of the Cowley Fathers, we are learning how to use the body as an act of prayer, the dance as a reflection upon living, the limbs as conveying stillness and themes of reflection. Through the writings on Christian Yoga (especially I would commend *Christian Yoga* by Fr. Déchanet), we are beginning to appreciate the importance of this training if we are to offer our whole selves to the reality of God in our time of reflection and in our day-to-day living.

This excerpt from Déchanet's book puts the point better than I could myself:

In fact I shall only profit by this "communication" from on high if I bring myself into harmony with God, and if, the whole day long, total communion with the divine will accords in me with the sacrament of communion. If certain ways of holding the body, certain attitudes and physical exercises by their nature promote this attitude in my soul and make it easier to receive graces, then this is a clear instance of the kind of link already discussed. Here, at a personal level, is a practical example of how the body is redeemed.

The same holds good if, in order to make my praying purer, I carry out some exercises beforehand, or if I adopt for meditation one of the postures well known in the East for promotiong concentration of the spirit and inner recollectedness.

In doing this, my intention is not to compel the supernatural, any more than it is to put all manner of acrobatics in the place of dispositions of the heart; nor is it to obtain by mechanical and artificial means what can only be the fruit of a sincere piety and a generosity of soul that appeals to divine Love. On the contrary it is simply to create around me an atmosphere of calm, peace, and silence, and especially to establish harmony between body, soul and spirit so that nothing in me shall hinder the working of grace. In short, I make use of a means, genial in its banality, of recollecting myself in the true sense of the word—of gathering myself together, of possessing myself, of having complete control of myself, so as to hand myself wholly over to God.[4]

In the next chapter certain simple exercises of breathing and posture are discussed which will contribute to the experience of contemplative prayer.

THE STAGES OF CONTEMPLATIVE PRAYER

The stages of contemplative prayer have been the same through the ages. They have been described as the Way of Purgation, the Way of Illumination, the Way of Union or the Unitive Life. Louis Bouyer in his great work *Introduction to Spirituality* describes them as the "ages of the spiritual life." St. John of the Cross describes them as the stages through which the soul passes in its approach to God. These stages of Christian living are not just to be experienced in the times of reflection or contemplative prayer but also in the processes of ordinary living or what I have called the Prayer of Involvement. To experience the reality of unity with God involves not just what happens in the quietness of prayer, but it is a transformation of one's entire life. Nevertheless it is valuable to see these three stages as guides to the way in which we approach our times of silence. They conform to the three requirements of contemplative prayer already outlined.

1. *The Way of Purgation:* If we desire to find the truth of things, where shall we find it? The answer of Christ is quite clear: "The kingdom of God is within you" (Luke 17:21). But how do we get to that reality through all the shams, the roles, the facades, the unrealities which have become ourselves? That is the basic issue of the Way of Purgation. Robert Browning puts it well:

> Truth is within ourselves. . . .
> There is an inmost centre in us all,
> Where truth abides in fullness; and around,

Wall upon wall, the gross flesh hems it in,
This perfect, clear perception—which is truth.

We need to penetrate through this "wall upon wall," which is not necessarily the "gross flesh" but the perverted and pressurized experiences of life by which we have been conditioned.

Let us remember, however, in practicing the Way of Purgation that we are always penetrating through the levels of consciousness to that deep consciousness within ourselves which is God. We must start with the conscious recognitions of what life has done to us. As we get deeper and deeper into ourselves we shall first find the costliness, the darkness, the insecurity of releasing our hold on much of what we have thought valuable. Ultimately, through the turning inwards, we shall find the center of life which is God and by which the different pulls of life may be resolved. As Dame Julian of Norwich puts it: "To mount to God is to enter into oneself. For he who inwardly entereth in and penetrateth into himself gets above and beyond himself and truly mounts to God." Always our search will be for reality. Through the "wall upon wall" of the pseudo, the role-playing, the facades, the masks, to that "I am that I am." This is what truly *is,* and is what we mean by God. And because that truly *is* is essentially personal, the search must lead through the levels of the personal.

Interestingly, the ways of psychology and psychiatry recently are more closely approaching the ways of prayer. Psychiatry has come increasingly to recognize that real problems do not revolve around battles with impulses and instincts but are concerned with personal reality experienced and grown in the medium of personal relationships. On one hand, we had those behaviorist psychologists who use aversion therapies to make people conform by mechanistic means to what society wants (e.g., the so-called reconditioning of the homosexual by pictures that excited his feelings and drugs that made him vomit).

On the other side, we had early Freudianism through which life was seen as a struggle to control or sublimate impulses and aggressions. Psychoanalysis focused on the distortions of personal relations rather than the ways by which we become whole, more on mental illness rather than on "abundant living." But now it is recognized more and more that the root of the problem is not the control of unruly impulses, still less an anti-personal, mechanistic attempt to make people conform, but rather to develop the growth of true selfhood, of basic wholeness as a person.

This concern is equally the motivation which lies behind prayer as a search for the reality of the self. That religious thought and psychological thought are drawing more closely together is a healthy development, whether this is or is not explicitly recognized, for we are now entering upon a new trust in relationship between psychiatrists and priests which did not previously exist. In the local hospital where I am chaplain to the psychiatric wards, I am now invited to take part as an equal in the group therapy and in the staff consultations with doctors, nurses, and occupational therapists. This would not have happened a few years ago. Hopefully, modern psychiatry may contribute to persons exploring in search of the true self, and this may more easily lead to the ways of prayer.

As one of the dimensions of the Way of Purgation, we need to make a conscious effort to recognize what life has done to us. To do this, we need to assess as objectively as we can the pressures which are upon us and their conditioning effect. How far am I motivated by the class or social background in which I live? Peter L. Berger in *The Noise of Solemn Assemblies* made the remark that the American church seems to identify the Christian gospel with the American way of life. If this is true, then how far do I regard values which may simply be middle-class or working-class values as if they were an expression of the Christian way of life? Can I identify the role or

mask which is being set for me by other people and how
far is my life a self-conscious identification with that
role? (For example, many people have a role for a priest
which would reduce him to the status of a nonbeing—
he is not to be difficult, not to lose his temper, not to
offend, not to say anything that will ever hurt anyone's
feelings, not to be anything but persistently "nice" and
"charming." Is this not a state of nonbeing rather than
true humanity?) How far can I recognize that my security
is threatened by status, by the world's estimate of success
and failure, by different groups in my neighborhood? To
what extent does prejudice or fear determine my attitude
to social misfits, people of other races, the sexually devi-
ant? These are the kinds of questions which if faced
honestly will help me assess my opinions and my values
in life.

Sometimes even the simplest things like political opinions or attitudes toward material possessions will speak
volumes to the truth about myself. I well remember a
discussion among a group of middle-class people in a
rather pleasant residential district. The question of attitudes toward immigrants of other races came up, and
all were speaking with praiseworthy liberality. Then a
house agent in their midst said, "Do you know why there
are practically no racial minorities in your area? It is
because house agents discourage the buying of houses in
this area by these people. But I take it from your liberality
that you would wish us to discontinue this practice?"
Immediately there was an embarrassed silence—then
various people started talking about house values and
their possible deterioration!

Again do we find that our professed Christian desires
are really at variance with our actual desires for life?
There is a telling phrase in the Psalms, "Thou gavest them
their hearts' desires and sent leanness withal into their
souls" (Psalm 106:15). How terribly true this phrase is.
Often we do, in fact, receive what we really desire, not
what we feel we ought to desire, and the result is that

our whole personalities become dwarfed and stunted. John Burnaby writes, "God's children may not approach their Father with a feigned devotion fearing to tell him what they truly want. I am to face with all the honesty I can achieve the real truth about my desires, to wrestle with the sham of professing desires which are not really mine. The schooling of desire is indeed prayer." [5] It is no good praying for humility if what I really want is power and success; it is no good praying for the guidance of the Holy Spirit if what I really want is to persuade someone to accept my own ideas; it is no good praying for love if what I really want is simply to go to bed with someone. Through prayer we can move from the world of fantasy to reality. Yet how do I know when I am in the world of reality rather than fantasy? Only insofar as my dreams accord with my actions and my will; otherwise they remain in the clouds—a land of feigned professions and wishful thinking.

In the Way of Purgation, there is also a second step by which we begin to penetrate to a deeper level. Even though I try to recognize as completely and honestly as I can the results of the human, sociological, and environmental pressures upon me, I need a measure of assessment by which I can penetrate to the deeper reality of my own being. The answer to how I know where the true reality of myself as a human being lies is given in Ephesians, "Until we all attain to the unity of the faith and of the knowledge of the Son of God to mature manhood, to the measure of the stature of the fulness of Christ" (Ephesians 4:13, RSV). If my true reality is the divinity within me, then obviously the measure of that true humanity lies in the One who "first conclusively fulfills the conditions of a humanity, namely to be organically united to God and fulfilled by the coinherence of God" (Nels Ferré).

Jesus is the fulfilled human being, but he did not begin with the transformed nature. He began where we all begin—with ordinary human nature. Otherwise there would have been no possibility of our finding union with him. What a false and unhelpful picture religion has often painted of the earthly life of Christ—as if he had none of the normal human desires and longings and temptations, as if he never expressed his emotions of anger, love, dislike, or contempt (there is no biblical evidence that he *liked* the Pharisees, and the only remark made upon the king of his country was one of contempt, "Go and tell that fox"), as if the struggles of Jesus were a make-believe in which he knew all the time that some foreordained "divinity" would make it come to a happy ending. It is not surprising that human beings have felt an unbridgeable gap existed between this perfect figure and their own drives and experiences of life.

Rather, in the human life of Jesus we see what a truly human person would be, an individual wholly and consistently open to all the possibilities of the environment and the world in which he lived, to all the demands and possibilities of other people as he meets them, and to the reality of God met in the midst of life and in other persons. Now in the ever-living Christ we all partake in this reality. It is the reality for which we are destined and in which we shall find our fulfillment, but in our nature as in his, it is not a fixed, static state. It is a gradually emerging and maturing pattern of life.

2. *The Way of Illumination:* When we begin to penetrate to this level of reality—the level at which we begin to measure ourselves by the stature of Christ—we shall experience a sense of darkness. This comes as a common trial to everyone who would really seek to know ultimate reality—God himself. The darkness occurs for three reasons:

First, the fullness of Christ living in me comes only through death. I do not mean a physical death, but a death to the clinging to the security of material desires, possessions, and fantasies without which there can be no resurrection, no true abundance of living. Christ very truly said, "For where your treasure is, there will your heart be also" (Matthew 6:21, RSV). For most of us, our treasures are very firmly rooted in some kind of security which we can find in the world of sensible things or persons. We are rooted in the idea of success achieved through the effort of what we call "getting on in the world." When I was visiting in America, someone said to me, "In America there is only one goal—success. The basic reason why in the States there is no welfare state is that it would encourage dependence upon others, encourage those who have failed to find support. There must be no failures in America." Therefore, to set aside what one has spent one's life in desiring is to feel very alone, unsupported, and in the dark.

Even from my human loves I have to learn detachment if I am to find God. "If any one comes to me and does not hate his own father and mother . . . and even his own life, he cannot be my disciple" (Luke 14:26, RSV). As Trevor Huddleston said when he had to face the costliness of obeying the command to leave the Africans he had loved:

> Detachment is only real if it involves loving; loving to the fullest extent of one's nature—but recognizing at the same time that such love is set in the context of a supernatural love of God. Then when the moment of surrender, of parting, comes, one has a worthwhile offering to make: an offering which is the love and affection of all the years, for all those one has known; it has some meaning, like the costly ointment poured over the feet of Christ. And it is costly too.[6]

Moreover, knowing the will of God in the present highly technological world becomes increasingly complex and confusing. Many people have said to me, "The Christian faith was more easily seen and preached in the simple world of pre-industrial times, but what does it mean to follow the way of Christ as an executive in industry, as an advertising consultant, as a shop steward, as a town planner?" The more sincerely the Christian wishes to love God the more perplexed he is as to what that discipleship means, what he must cease to desire, and how he can cease to desire in his present situation. It is truly a darkness for which we need to find illumination.

The second darkness as we move nearer to the center of our being will be the darkness resulting from wrestling with the uncertainties of faith and belief. In this secular age, it seems a very difficult commitment to stake all upon belief in God. We have to pray in an age which does not know God, which is turned from him and closed to him. We are ourselves inevitably affected, though as Christians we have no particular loyalty to our present impersonal and materialistic civilization. In an age characterized largely by unbelief, in which statements of faith are treated with skepticism difficult to combat, the contemplative has to learn to be open to God, to pass through the death of disbelief to the resurrection of a faith, based not upon argument but upon a more direct and intuitive knowledge of reality. This will not be easy. It will bring us into conflict with darkness and despair, and a lust for power and domination. The struggle may subject us to the laughter and scorn of the skeptics as Gerontius on his journey to heaven was subjected to the laughter and scorn of the demons in hell. Many a Christian minister and lay person feel the darkness of this sense of futility and powerlessness as they survey their empty churches and recognize how little they count in the world of affairs.

With the centuries the Christian mental background has been eroded and to a large extent replaced by the scientific and factual world view. Much gain as well as loss occurred in this change, and we must and should welcome the advances in understanding, healing, discovery of truth which the secular city has brought. But as a result of the climate of opinion, reflection on Christian truth is now as likely to lead to uncertainty and doubt as to deeper faith and commitment. Even within the Christian church today, there are more questions asked than answers given. This questioning is good, but faith has to find a more secure anchor than simply intellectual knowledge. Then living with uncertainty as a characteristic of life can be something not to be avoided but welcomed. For this reason, many people today are searching for an inner experience to make good the lack of social support in their faith.

The dark night described by St. John of the Cross is still strikingly relevant to much of the modern search for reality and meaning in life. Christians are living in a kind of corporate dark night. St. John of the Cross says that the loss of the old landmarks and guides leads to a new and intuitive way of knowing God. He calls it the way of faith based on the unknowability of God, who is reached not by intellect but by intuition, by silent waiting upon the certainty of his love—the only certainty we have. But along with this silent waiting come feelings of emptiness and unreality. The old landmarks have lost their meaning; the old religious ideas have gone dead; the church and its worship is boring and meaningless.

I was talking to a woman of great intelligence and integrity in our congregation only the other day. She was saying how everything in which she had believed seemed to have gone dead, save her inner feeling that God is there, and that there is somewhere a deep meaning behind life. She would not have understood what I meant if I had told her that she was going through the dark night of the soul, but this is basically what is happening to her. I believe her intuitive sense of faith and commitment to what at present she cannot even describe or name will bring her through this sense of death to new life. I do not know whether she will or will not return to the church, but I am convinced that she will find a real union with God.

The third and most complete darkness is the darkness of the loss of God himself. Bonhoeffer speaks from his situation of having to learn to live without God, as if God were not there. What this means is that if a person is to reach his own ultimate reality of becoming one with God, he or she has first to experience a sense of the loss of God. This loss is the ultimate test of faith. Perhaps the nearest human analogy is that of learning to live in the love of another human being who has been withdrawn from my presence either by death or distance or because his own life and love has been given to another. At first I shall experience a great sense of darkness and loss, and I shall need to mourn. Then I shall discover that my love remains for him/her and I must learn to live life again as it was lived in his presence, with joy, with hope, with caring for others. Insofar as I learn again to live in love, I shall relive in his life, and the sense of his presence will return as something with which I am now eternally in union.

We must always remember that even Jesus himself could not experience the ultimate reunion with God until he had gone through the dark night of "My God, my God, why hast thou forsaken me?" (Matthew 27:46, RSV) St. Paul most wonderfully expresses this same sense of the darkness in the beautiful words of 1 Corinthians 13: "For now we see through a glass, darkly, but then face to face: now I know in part; but then shall I know even as also I am known."

St. John of the Cross sums up all this stage of darkness in the following words:

> We may say that there are three reasons for which this journey made by the soul to union with God is called night. The first has to do with the point from which the soul goes forth, for it has gradually to deprive itself of desire for all the worldly things which it possessed, by denying them to itself; the which denial and deprivation are, as it were, night to all the senses of man. The second reason has to do with the mean, or the road along which the soul must travel to this union—that is, faith, which is likewise as dark as night to the understanding. The third has to do with the point to which it travels—namely God, who, equally, is dark night to the soul in this life. These three nights the soul must pass through in order that it may come to Divine union with God.[7]

In the quietness of our reflection, we shall seek God's illumination of these dark nights by an understanding of the scriptures. Our reading will be motivated by the desire to find in the Bible the disclosure of the word of God in relation to the various kinds of darkness in which we find ourselves. Our faith will not be a search to find in the Bible certain and dogmatic answers but rather to discover the questions with which God is striking through the darkness to us, and the flashes of insight which he is allowing us to have so that we may grasp him intuitively as we endeavor to make some sense of the mazes of life in which we live.

3. *The Unitive Way:* The last and highest stage of both prayer and living is what is called the Way of Union. It is difficult to describe and even more difficult to experience or attain. Perhaps the easiest way to describe this state is to observe that it is the state in which our whole personality has been so transformed by our penetration through reality to ever-deeper reality (both of reflection and living) that we have now in a very real sense become God. In this state I have so been filled with creative love that I have been merged into, absorbed into God, and in so doing I have at last become myself. Christ knew what this meant when he said, "He who has seen me has seen the Father" (John 14:9, RSV). St. Paul knew what this union meant when he said, "I live; yet not I, but Christ liveth in me" (Galatians 2:20).

Happold sums up the state of union with God in this way:

> When a man can be said to have passed through the state of Illumination to that of Union it is difficult to determine. . . . . We need not, however, try to be too precise. It is sufficient to say that, when a man follows the Mystic Way to its end, this is the state which is attained. The death of selfhood is complete, an utter transformation of personality has taken place, so that a new creature is born, a new and permanent change of consciousness has been brought about. The soul . . . is 'oned' with God.[8]

Whether anyone other than Christ has ever fully attained this permanent union with God, I do not know, but it is sufficient to say that there are means by which we can recognize when it is beginning to happen in us. The last stage of prayer cannot, however, be taught as can the earlier stages, for it becomes a gift of God to the one who has persisted through the dark night and the purgations in his determination to find the true reality and meaning of life and of himself.

It is also important to understand that when we come to the ultimate stage of reflection, we are back again in the world of involvement. The only way by which we can form any assessment of the person who has achieved some degree of union with God is through his attitudes towards the world and its people. A high degree of union may have been found through much silent searching for ultimate reality, much waiting in stillness upon God, but it will only be disclosed as such when the prayer of reflection becomes the prayer of involvement, when the result of this transformation of personality is seen in its encounters with the world. As in Christ, so in us, the road from Nazareth to Jerusalem, from Bethlehem to the Cross, is the road in which the encounters are found where the divine union is seen, in daily living not in withdrawal from the world.

The writings of Teilhard de Chardin bring this out clearly. For him union with God was not through withdrawal from the activity of the world (although he would, of course, have found every reason for the deep reflection and contemplation of which we have been speaking) but through a dedicated, integrated, Christo-centric absorption in it. Not only man but human activity in all its forms is capable of divination and of divine union.

Now I wish to give some practical help in the practice of the earlier stages of contemplative prayer. The next chapter is devoted to the consideration of some exercises in contemplative prayer which I hope will be of value.

CHAPTER 4

Some Exercises in Contemplative Praying

SUGGESTIONS FOR FINDING AND
KEEPING SILENCE

1. Find the time of the day when silence is most likely to be possible for you. For someone engaged in business, it may be during the lunch hour in some nearby building or church (many use Southwark Cathedral in this way, standing as it does in the heart of London); for the housewife, it may well be when husband is at work and children are at school; for others, the beginning of the day, immediately before or after breakfast, may be the best time.

2. Learn to practice silence in the midst of noise (e.g., when sitting in a bus or waiting for the subway) by listening quite deliberately to the outside noises. Instead of thinking of them as getting in the way, concentrate on these outside noises, whatever they are, and realize that they represent the activities of human life. In this way one is mentally bringing other people into the silence one is trying to reach. Soak in the noises until they no longer distract but have become one with you in the search for reality.

3. Concentrate on some background noise like the ticking of a clock. I am writing this book in the house of

a friend where in the background there is a wall clock steadily ticking away. By listening to this, I am finding silence, for there is something in it of eternity, something that steadies the chatter within me.

4. Begin to concentrate totally and completely on your own breathing; become conscious that your breathing is your life deep within, is symbolic of the life you are seeking, that God is the creator of the life which is expressed through your breathing. Become conscious of breathing in and out (Father—in, Jesus—breath held, Spirit—out). This helps one to be still and to begin to enter into the depths of oneself.

5. Sometimes a repetitive phrase like the Eastern mantras or the Orthodox Jesus Prayer contributes to stillness: "Lord Jesus Christ, Son of God, have mercy upon us"; "Returning to one's roots is known as stillness" (Lao Tzu). For some a background of appropriate music leads to stillness.

6. Look fixedly at something: a curtain, a picture, a crucifix, a lighted candle, your hands. Keeping one's gaze quite still and focused on one point or object makes for concentrated silence within as well as without.

All these and many others are ways by which, through the practice of some fixed point of concentration or deliberate choice of place or noise, one is learning both exterior and interior silence.

THE PREPARATION OF THE BODY

In many ways, the body may be trained to be alert, attentive, and yet relaxed so that the stillness of the body contributes to the inward search of the mind and heart. Part of the routine of rising can include the training of the body for alertness and attention. Immediately on rising, take a cold shower or bath. You may shudder at this, but my own experience is that it contributes considerably to a feeling of alertness and well-being. Then while still in the nude (for it is valuable to feel that freedom of the body which is never felt when clothed), do some simple exercises. I have found the following of particular value.

1. The control and consciousness of breathing is an aid in contemplation. Stand with legs apart, draw the stomach in, hold the breath, slowly expel the breath. Draw the breath in for a count of three, hold for a count of twelve, breathe out for a count of six. Do this several times and establish a rhythm in which you are consciously listening to your breathing. Then associate thoughts of God with your breathing. As you breathe in, think "God the Father who created me and all people in his image." As you hold the breath, think "Jesus, live within me this day; Christ in me and I in Christ." As you expel the breath, think "Holy Spirit, come with me into my world and all that I must do this day."

2. Certain postures can be used to express the relationship of body, mind, and spirit.

The Obeisance: Stand with legs apart and slowly touch the floor with the flat of one's hands without bending the knees. Combine this with thoughts of adoration or the intial phrases of "Our Father."

The Tree: Transfer all the weight of the body to the left leg. Lift the right leg, sliding it up along the left to knee height, then grasp it and pull it along the thigh until the heel rests deep in the lower part of the left groin. Join the hands in front of the chest and remain in this position for a few seconds. Next raise the arms slowly to form an arch above your head. Stay for a few seconds holding your breath; then lower and repeat the procedure with the other leg.

As you lift your hands above your head, think "All my heart goes out to thee, O Lord." As you hold the position, think "Search me out, O Lord; direct me and teach me thy paths" or other suitable phrases of harmony between ourselves and the ways of reality.

The Bent Bow: Lying flat on the stomach, bend the knees fully so that the calves lie close to the thighs. Stretch back the arms, grasp firmly first one ankle then the other. Spread the knees slightly sideways, then push strongly against your hands with your legs. Your body makes a bent bow. This is a most suitable exercise for thoughts of direction and sending forth—the shooting of myself into the coming day with the reality of God within as my power.

Many other exercises of this kind are found in *Christian Yoga* by Déchanet. These are the ones I have personally found most valuable. The effect of these exercises is that the greater harmony of body gained is itself an aid to harmony of spirit and mind in concentration. Because of the interaction of body and spirit, a harmonious and well-balanced body will help toward a harmonious and well-balanced soul; a body unregulated and uncomfortable will produce a distracted and ill-ordered spirit. The effects of the breathing exercises are not only that they calm and bring a feeling of well-being, but more importantly they enable you to feel more detached, more able to reflect, and to focus attention. People have dwelt much on how to keep the mind concentrated, but the bodily side has been ignored. To pray with real searching, one must be self-possessed, in control of oneself, and calm. To reach this state, postures of body and control of breathing bring about an attunement which rebounds deeply on the inner life.

EXERCISES IN CONTEMPLATIVE PRAYER

I list here a few examples of possible contemplative prayer.

1. A Prayer of Purgation
   Preparation:
   a. Practice one of the techniques of silence—see above.
   b. Sit quietly, body straight, feet firmly on the floor, hands resting lightly on the knees.
   c. Concentrate on some object and draw out all the

thoughts that occur as you look at the object (this will put you in a concentrated mood).

Material for Reflection (the words in quotes are from St. John of the Cross):

"In order to have pleasure in everything
Desire to have pleasure in nothing."

Reflection:

a. What do I most desire? Can I desire to have nothing? Can I stand aside from that desire and look deeply at it? Could I dispense with that desire before God?
Silence

b. "In order to arrive at possessing everything
Desire to possess nothing."
How much do my possessions mean to me? Am I simply concerned with the necessities of life or am I "hung up" on possessions? Can I look deeply into myself and discover the truth?
Silence

c. "In order to arrive at being everything
Desire to be nothing."
What does being nothing mean? Does it not mean just being myself, which is being everything, rather than being a role which I present before others? What are the facades, the masks behind which I hide?
Silence

d. "In order to arrive at knowing everything
Desire to know nothing."
What does desire to know nothing mean? Is it simply to rest in the love of God rather than to seek to find a reason for everything? Where lies the certainty of my own knowledge of truth?
Silence

Conclusion: "The kingdom of heaven is within me" —but is it? "Lord Jesus Christ, son of God, have mercy upon me a sinner."

2. A Prayer of Purgation

Preparation: Same as before.

Material for Reflection: The light and the darkness within me.

Jesus said: "I am the light of the world."

"Christ as the light, make thy light illumine my subconscious being, lead me from the unreal to the real, from darkness to light, from death to life."

Reflection:

a. Lead me from the unreal to the real. Where are the unrealities of my own life? the shams, the window-dressing, the pseudo in work and in personal relationships?

   Silence

b. Lead me from the darkness to the light. What are the darknesses of my life? the lack of the fruits of the spirit—love, joy, peace, etc.? What are the fears and insecurities of my life?

   Silence

c. Lead me from death to life. What is spelling out death in my own life? What is destructive rather than creative in my relationships at work or at home? What do I mean by love?

   Silence

Conclusion: Will the darkness in me reject the light or will I allow the light to reject the darkness?

Prayer: Lord Jesus Christ,

Lead me from the unreal to the real—by honesty.

Lead me from the darkness to the light—by truth and purity.

Lead me from death to life—by love.

3. A Prayer of Illumination

Preparation: As before.

Material for Reflection: Knowing myself in Christ, responsible human living.

Reflection:

a. I am made in the image of God—the image of God is truly reflected in Christ—therefore "I welcome you, Christ; come and abide with me?" But Christ may reply, "I cannot abide in your heart—there is no room."
Who is at present dwelling too much in my heart?
Silence

b. What is at present dwelling too much in my heart?
Silence

c. Where do I find the presence of Christ?
"Do I not meet you everywhere I go?
Do I not find you dwelling in my brother's eyes?
Do I not hear you speaking in the earth's sad voice?
Do I not feel you in a mother's loving care?"
(adapted from Buddhist poem)

d. How can I take Christ into my work today?
Silence

e. How can I take Christ into the deepest human relationships I have?
Silence

f. How can I take Christ into the needs of others? Do I know them?
Silence

Conclusion: As you do the exercise of the Bent Bow, think, "O Loving One, with you in my heart, shoot me into your world today; take this my earthly life and let it be reborn in you. Unite me with you today."

I hope that the various exercises I have given are a help to the practice of contemplative prayer and suggest ways for you to proceed. Useful background material for such prayer will be found in Part 3 of *Prayer and Meditation* and in the anthology entitled *Mysticism,* both by F. C. Happold and published by Penguin Books.

CHAPTER 5
Praying with the Bible

Earlier I wrote that finding the will of God today is difficult because of the complexity of the situations in which we live. Because of this difficulty, praying with the Bible becomes important. But if it is to be an effective way to the understanding of reality, certain misconceptions about the Bible itself must be examined.

First, the Bible cannot be seen as a sort of copybook which sets out a neat series of answers to the problems of the individual in his world. Some Christians seem to go to the Bible in this spirit. In discussions about various problems, texts are quoted as if the text itself, isolated from its context and without reference to the whole setting of the situation, would provide some sort of mechanical answer. Anyone who has tried to have a discussion with certain kinds of fundamentalist sects will know exactly what I mean. Indeed, a certain longing for "answers" is understandable in a world where it would be pleasant to have ready-made solutions. This would make life much easier, but persons attempting to penetrate through to reality could not possibly be satisfied with such shallowness of thinking.

Secondly, the Bible is less than helpful if approached on a mechanistic or literal level. If I am so conditioned by the world in which I live that even my knowledge of God must be factual and literal, then I shall not only be involved in endless difficulties of how to make one set of stories and sayings cohere with another, but I shall be abdicating both my reason and my sense of wonder in order to bolster up a childish and ludicrous faith. The Bible contains such a lively dialogue with God that all manner of providential occurrences, epiphanies, and miracles are recorded which we cannot equate with the normal routine of existence as we know it. Any attempt to straitjacket it in the fundamentalist fashion will bring us into richly deserved ridicule from a skeptical world.

Thirdly, the great dogmas of faith enshrined in the Bible are not objects of faith to be accepted or rejected or even primarily to be intellectually understood, but rather are channels through which one may be led to truths which are intuitively assimilated. Like symbols of spiritual illumination, or expressions of eternal realities, they are described, as only eternal realities can be, through poetry and story, boats for a voyage of discovery, maps to guide one on a journey—the journey through life. If viewed in this way, the great beliefs of the Christian faith—Incarnation, Passion, Resurrection, Ascension —become symbols and illuminations of living. They cease to be things which a Christian is expected to believe. Rather they are known from the experience of daily living.

Finally, in reading the Bible as a search for reality, one needs always to have in mind the world of race riots, unemployment, overcrowding, starvation, motorways, advertisement pressures, pop festivals, sex symbols, drugs. The theology which does not speak to such a world is a theology which is dead. God is not dead, but many of the ways in which we try to define him are well and truly dead and should long since have been buried if theology is to be concerned with what is real and what is meant by coming alive in the presence of God.

With this background, what kind of praying with the

Bible brings illumination from God for his world and us?

First, I would suggest that we spread before us the particular situation for which we seek to find illumination. This may be done either personally or corporately. Often biblical study will be best done with others so that there is a sharing of the intuitions gained both on the various ramifications of the situations and on the spiritual illumination received through the study of the Bible.

I once worked with groups of lay people who came together on the weekend to thresh out some of their difficult problems of illumination in the world in which they worked or lived. Often such groups would be people engaged in the same work and thus facing similar problems in their work. I remember a group of advertisers facing the relationship between truth and pressure in advertising, a group of executives in industry wrestling with the effects of automation and redundancy upon persons in their employ, a group of shop stewards asking questions of loyalty, a group of architects and town planners realizing with dismay the appalling effects of their building and planning upon the lives of people. The problem would be spread out, probably symbolized into a case study through which the details of the problem could be seen or maybe through a role play in which some of the difficulties could be articulated. Then we would turn to the thinking of the Bible not just in some random selection, but in careful choices of scripture which had some disclosure to make to the situation in question. First in silence, then in common thinking, we would wrestle with the meaning of the disclosure which God had to make to us. Gradually, not by intellect so much as by intuition, we would discern some solutions to the problems. In this study I would recommend Ian Ramsey's *Religious Language*.

In this way, prayer (in the above situation, the study of the situation, the silence of reflection, the study of the disclosures of God through the Bible are all equally a part of prayer) works in relation to the Bible when illuminanation is sought for the situations of a complex world, when the light of the word of God is brought to bear upon the muddle and darkness of knowing where decision and commitment lie. The word *disclosure* is the important word for the study of the Bible and the praying of the Bible is not the study of the "answers" of God but God giving depth and new reality to the understanding of a situation. The situation becomes alive, for what was dark becomes illumined with the reality. A new dimension comes to the situation, and I, as the seeker, become more alive to the full understanding of it because an activity other than my own has met it—the activity of God which is ultimate reality. What was basically unreal, a muddle of darkness, becomes a situation in which I, in union with God, can act and illumine.

Perhaps what is happening is that the various stages of the spiritual life—the purgative, the illuminative, and the unitive have become not so much successive stages as expressions of different inroads into an understanding of life. The prophetic writings of the Bible are indeed models of this. The prophet first sees as a great darkness or muddle the situation of life in Israel or Judah. Then what is needed by way of purging, tearing down, and exposing is disclosed to him. Finally the searchlight of the illumination of God's disclosure is brought to bear so that at last there may be the unity of God and man meeting in a relation of mutual activity.

Indeed it is interesting symbolically that many of the disclosures of God come in the wilderness, perhaps suggesting that it is only when we are truly in the wilderness, stripped of the supports, the facades, the roles, the pressures, that we can begin to see God's revealing of reality. That it is God's disclosure is always certain to the prophet who intuitively relates all his judgments on the situation to "Thus saith the Lord."

The other kind of praying with the Bible is reflective meditation in which the person ponders upon the sayings of Christ until he experiences leaps of understanding and flashes of insight into life. In this way I have found personally that such phrases as "I am the way, the truth, and the life," "I am the bread of life," and many others have lit up for me. In a new way I discovered that in Christ I have life abundant as well as eternal, here as well as hereafter, that there is nothing the world has to offer which can be compared to the joy, the peace, and the love of that life, and yet that I shall only discover that joy, that peace, and that love through and in the world. As Teilhard de Chardin so beautifully put it, "Christianity is not, as it is sometimes presented and practiced, an additional burden of observances and obligations to weigh down and increase the already heavy load, or to multiply the already paralyzing ties of our life in society. It is, in fact, a soul of immense power which bestows significance and beauty and a new lightness upon what we are already doing." [1]

This kind of intuitive understanding of the reality we are offered awakens and deepens our responsiveness to God, our saying yes to him. So out of this kind of praying with the Bible comes that sense of commitment which is the result of discernment. In fact, one might say that discernment, disclosure, and commitment are the words which spell out what praying with the Bible means.

Powerful symbols are called up which can speak to the depths of our life when we pray using the Bible with imagination. Jesus, crucified and risen, is the embodied symbol of God reaching down to the region of our deepest fears, facing the worst we can imagine, making himself vulnerable, yet remaining always free, identifying himself with us as our brother in order to make us one with God. In the biblical symbols, we recognize the bridge between the conscious personality and its unconscious depths. This is so vividly expressed by the names given to Christ in the New Testament: Messiah —my hopes; Son of Man, Son of God—my own reality; King and Lord—my power; Savior and Mediator—my need; the "I AM'S" of St. John—my life.

CHAPTER 6
The Prayer of the Now

In the past I have given more emphasis to the Prayer of the Now, the prayer of involvement in life itself, rather than to the reflective side of prayer. In this book I have reversed this emphasis. I do this not because I consider the prayer of involvement less important, but because I have discovered that we can fulfill the active side of people only if we give far more attention to the contemplative side. The active side of persons needs the contemplative side to resolve the deep questions of meanings, goals, and directions. Without contemplation we are simply blown to and fro by every new wind. Without contemplation we have no roots, and without roots there can be no real security, no real growth, no real fulfillment. A rhythm of activity and passivity is necessary for full living.

Therefore, in this chapter, I want to indicate the kinds of perspective on life which will follow from a serious emphasis on contemplation and reflection. These are shared in the belief that out of our times of disengagement will come the resources for involvement in the world.

COURAGE TO ACT

It is in the real world of persons and events that reflection and contemplation become the reality of action.

The meaning and reality of the Christian life is not expressed within the walls of a church but in actual day-to-day living. The city is where the union between God and man takes place. The stuff of life—problems of housing, race, hunger, transportation, business, integrity, civil rights, education, industry, family—these provide the raw material for the Holy Spirit to dwell within and to direct. In fact, the sacred and the secular cannot be separated for all life is spiritual. The true life of the Spirit is experienced when all activities of life are rooted in the reality of love.

This life in the Spirit is possible because the time of reflection allows us to penetrate through the fantasies of life to reality, and prayer gives the courage to act when the reality becomes clear. In fact, direct action may also enable us to see through fantasy to reality. For example, I have a friend who has a vision of building a lovely home one day where he will welcome all his friends. At the present moment this is fantasy, but it will become reality when he has the courage to act—to start choosing the home, to work consciously towards the building of that home, to sacrifice time and money, to furnish it, and above all to welcome the people into it. Then the fantasy will have become reality because the action will follow the reflection.

A part of the courage to act is knowing that the search for reality always involves the death of many of our securities, but that there will be in the attitude of one who is praying life a certain freedom from those securities and a certain willingness to take risks. A life of involvement grows from a commitment to the unknown without the need to have certainty of faith and proof. In other words, the Prayer of the Now is built on a freedom and commitment in life which is born out of willingness to let go.

Something of the holiness which characterized the saint of old will be the characteristic of the new saint. I would define this holiness as a freedom from concern with success and ambition, a certain carelessness about material reward, a freedom to become aware of other people and an ability to respond to them, and a lack of fear of the judgment or criticism of others. This sense of commitment to the unknown enables persons to embark on new truth and new discoveries, to risk the uncharted rather than be content with the paths of safety.

A NEW CONSCIOUSNESS OF PROTEST

Inspite of the increasing unreality of life which an impersonal and technological world has brought us, union with God can bring new *consciousness* of living. Interestingly, Reich uses the word *consciousness* in *The Greening of America* to describe the new attitudes to life of those who are in protest in America. He says that there has evolved a Consciousness III to replace the Consciousness II of the public state. This Consciousness III has certain characteristics: liberation, the individual self being the only true reality, the absolute worth of every human being, the refusal to categorize and attribute comparative merit to human beings, the need to be true to oneself, the realization that the whole world is one family, the need to hope and have enthusiasm, the importance of the body, personal responsibility for the life around us. All these characteristics would be equally true of the individual who is praying his life. He, therefore, will be in continual protest against the depersonalization and dehumanizing of life which is going on around him; he will be an outsider to the world, a protester against life as he finds it in order to make life what it should be.

All in all, the deadliness of much life is the main reason many individuals find it difficult to find reality in living or find it difficult to express and feel love in the environment which is theirs. Necessarily we must learn and evaluate the results of the deadly routine of modern life. It might be helpful to read such books as Erich Fromm's

Escape from Freedom or *The Sane Society,* or David Riesman's *The Lonely Crowd.*

We have reason to ponder these questions: Can persons be individuals in an age of mass media, automation, urban agglomeration, and bureaucracy? Can the underprivileged person living with his whole family in one room practice any kind of reflection? Can a person of little education discover the way to penetrate through to reality? Can a lonely person find solitude as a means of knowing God? Only as we have understood and eventually protested against these conditions shall we take our praying out of a cozy middle-class religion into an area of reality. Only as we realize the incredible difficulty of the life of prayer and involvement in our world, can we then begin to affirm and describe how many yet manage to remain human, responsible, and alive. To understand reality is to know that the life of prayer is lived out as a protest against the deadness and inhumanity surrounding us.

THE HOPE OF THE FUTURE

Nevertheless the Prayer of the Now will not be in protest against the secular world as such but only against the perversions of that world. As Teilhard de Chardin has so clearly shown, the discoveries of modern science have revealed a future of unity in which all things are bound together in the providence of God. Earth itself is to be completed, and every scrap of human endeavor to perfect the earth should be seen as valuable in God's sight, necessary in fulfilling God's purposes in the unity of his whole creation. For the Christian, therefore, there exists an attitude of hope for the world, a deliberate looking forward to and working for God's kingdom to come on earth.

Because of this hope, the perspective of the prayer of life will be one of protest against all that is destructive in the movements of the world because of a belief in God's purposes of creative life. It is the death wish of modern civilization against which we protest. To use the words of John Lehmann: "The desire to be destroyed seemed no better than the desire to destroy; and as I had in the preceding years come to see that the latter arose in our time from a vacancy of belief, so now I saw the former as a direct result of the same despair." [1]

RESPONDING WITH REALITY

In the process of living out the prayer of involvement, the question of communication is often raised. How do I speak out my needs and feelings to God? There is no stereotyped form of speaking, but there seem to be natural moments when we speak out—when we feel happy, joyful, appreciative, pleased; when we are angry, exasperated or frustrated with life; when we are frightened, anxious, fearful.

It would indeed be a death-in-life if there were no moments when I felt thankful and expressed this to God. But it must be remembered that when I say "thank you" to God I am really learning what it is to appreciate life for myself and for others. I shall normally, therefore, express my appreciation to the persons who have given me the experience of happiness or joy. Indeed, one of the most necessary qualities of a life of reality is that we should learn to be far less critical and far more appreciative.

However, there is no reason to avoid honest, direct expressions of anger with God, no reason why we should not rage against God if we want to. Reality demands that, as in a family, I don't stand on ceremony. When I feel rage or frustration, then I must find release of it. Those who love me are quite willing to hear my feelings, whatever they are. As the Abbé Fénelon said, "If God bores you, tell him so." If for the moment, you hate God—tell him so. Elijah did, so did Teresa.

When I am fearful, a very simple "help me" is again the natural response of feeling. It might be addressed to God, or it might be addressed, if it were a wrestling of

personal difficulties of love and security of love, to another human being. Many a conversation in which difficulties of feelings, anxieties, and securities are faced and
shared becomes truly a prayer situation, because it is a
facing and sharing of reality.

So the Prayer of the Now is a living of life by certain
perspectives of courage, risk, protest, hope, and honesty.
All these perspectives are the result of the search for
reality so that life may be fully human. In the Prayer of
the Now, that search is made concrete through actions of
courage and hope and love so that we are now affirm-
ing God in every circumstance of life.

CHAPTER 7
The Prayer of Togetherness

Primarily, I have focused on personal prayer as a search for reality in life. However, as all persons live their life in various groups, it would be wrong to omit the Prayer of Togetherness, the sharing of reality expressed through a group of people. This can take place in a variety of settings such as learning groups or worshiping groups.

THE SMALL GROUP

Recently the small group has become more important because of the growing impersonality of modern society. This is especially true in large urban areas. We are realizing that a viable way to experience community and become more human in our togetherness is through the small group. In fact, the bigger the communities to which we belong, the more we need the support of smaller units or groups. People can and do get lost in the sheer size of our modern cities and become dehumanized. Christ himself in bringing the apostles together expressed the need of a small group to share the experiences of life. Perhaps today God is using the small group to keep persons human in a world where so much brings loss of self.

The small group can be an expression of prayer in various ways. The therapeutic group (prevalent in many psychiatric hospitals) is a group in which people share their problems and find their releases. In such a group persons may "speak the truth in love," give vent to their frustrations, let their feelings come into the open, experience the dark night of the soul together, know the pain of sharing their present identity in order to probe deeper into the reality of who they can be. The church itself would be more valuable to people if it could be such a releasing community instead of the artificially "nice" group it often tries self-consciously to be.

In group dynamics education, the learning group is a group which deliberately meets together to study their own behavior in order to learn about the life which goes on within groups. By so doing, they discover how to cope with groups in community living. In these types of experiences, with the help of trained observers, we can experience consciously how we behave to each other— our problems of leadership, domination, shyness, the disciplines of "when to shut up and when to speak up," how to live with the tensions and difficulties of others.

Through this kind of experience, we learn that decisions and the amount of discussion time will often depend not upon reason and logic but upon the feelings within the group for each other and for the subject under discussion. It has been said that in any council or committee as much will depend upon the "hidden agenda" within the hearts of the participants as on the written agenda before them. I recently experienced this in a very heated meeting at our own church because of a suggestion that we should sell our historic silver valued at twenty thousand pounds. At present this is locked in the vaults of a bank, but a concern for a more practical use of the money was causing quite a stir among the people. It was quite obvious that many at that meeting were not motivated by the reality of the situation but by a feeling of insecurity at letting go of possessions, or by a desire to retain the traditional at all costs. To be able to look at such feelings within a group was valuable.

In a similar way, experiments in observing the behavior of a large group will reveal the feelings of frustration at not being able to get into the debate, the tendency to be swayed by the herd, the anger and emotions roused by someone capable of manipulating feeling. In experiments involving several groups, one can experience the difficulties of communication between one group and another. All these training groups can give us valuable experience in understanding the very real difficulties of life within any community, both large and small. They express the true meaning of prayer by revealing how our inner realities affect our relationships with other people.

In our diocese various groups of clergy meet regularly in such groups as a learning experience. This is particularly valuable to clergy who rarely meet each other at this more human level. As the present Dean of Westminster once said, "It is often more difficult for the clergy to learn to love each other than to learn to love their parishioners." This is perhaps not surprising since each cleric tends to be a threat to his neighbor.

In the more structured discussion or Bible study group, the relationship between the gospel and daily living is threshed out by the participants. I have already mentioned this kind of group. As a framework for such a group I would suggest some guidelines:

- A limited time of meeting—perhaps eight sessions, then a break, and regrouping.
- A definite subject or biblical theme for each meeting, beginning with corporate reading or brief exposition by the group leader.
- Begin the study by sharing in small subgroups of twos and then in the larger group.
- Allow for a time of silence and reflection upon the theme and meaning elicited.
- Together explore how this disclosure affects your own life and environment.
- Possibly the focusing of the thinking into a shared prayer or a house Eucharist.

CORPORATE WORSHIP

The intention behind worship is the intention in the word *togetherness*. I would define this word in the way that Reich does in *The Greening of America*. He says *togetherness* is not an external conformity, nor a specific personal love relationship but rather " 'Together' expresses the relationship among people who feel themselves to be members of the same species, who are related to each other and to all of nature by the underlying order of being. People are 'together' when they experience the same thing in the same way." [1] This togetherness may be expressed in all kinds of ways—the togetherness of a holiday with friends, or a concert or pop festival, or a demonstration. But the togetherness of Christians lies in the common sharing of belief, the common expression of communion in Holy Communion, the experiencing of a common view of what is real and meaningful in life. All this is focused in worship, which has been well defined as "the reality of all that we are, offered to the reality of all that we know God to be." Perhaps, in other words, it is the offering of our pseudo-reality and the receiving of our true reality—"this is my body, this is my blood." Worship is a necessary focusing of that consciousness of reality which we personally experience in our time of reflection but now experience together with all who are bound in a common understanding of being.

Why then does worship often seem so unreal and so unrelated to life? Why does it cause a young man to remark, "I am profoundly interested in and excited by the understanding of God, the meaning of life, the reality of myself, but when I hear the word *church* it spells boredom for me"? Partly it is a crisis of communication, and partly that we have made it a crisis of irrelevance.

The crisis in communication arises from the fact that the communications medium has provided a type of perception radically different from that provided by the spoken or written word. As a common experience, perception of reality is achieved by direct participation, by involvement. Television brings the world right into one's room; news is not received by ear but by sight and by involvement with what is happening. This particularly affects the younger generation's attitude to worship. If someone of my generation missed church, he probably would have asked, "What did the preacher say?" Today the young person in our congregation says, "What happened?"

The word-package that constitutes most Protestant worship just isn't turned on for a generation accustomed to participation and involvement. Worship is not a focusing of reality as people understand reality today. It is noticeable that the churches in which there is this involvement of the whole person like many of the black churches, the Pentecostalist groups, and the strongly revivalist or ceremonialist churches are the churches which draw worshipers today. They have realized that if you want to move people spiritually you must also move them physically. But our problem is middle-class consciousness also. Metaphorically we "got shoes" and our respectability has been pinching us ever since!

We can see the crisis of irrelevance in that so much of our ideas of worship are dominated by ideas of churchmanship which died years ago and which have no relevance to modern generations. We live in a past where Protestantism stood for austerity and abhorrence of movement and ceremony and where Roman Catholicism represented incense, color, and theatre to be watched instead of participated in. Today this is increasingly not so. The Roman Catholics are often stark and barren; West Indian Protestants are colorful and "swinging." But we still carry on churchmanship divisions and discussions which are miles away from the conversation and interest of ordinary people.

What then do we need if our worship is to be a focusing of reality? First, we need to see worship as a *celebration of living* in which the response to life is a response of

the whole being—a response with the body as well as
with the mind and spirit. We need to use the dance, the
kiss, the touch, the clapping of hands, the gestures of
appreciation (or indeed the reverse—I know of one
church where a good sermon receives applause, a bad
one silence!). We need to let our worship express what
we are trying to say about life without getting bound up
with a traditional view of churchmanship. At times we
will be primarily expressing the austerities and asceticism
of life (e.g., in Lent, when we shall naturally let the
setting of worship speak to that austerity) but at other
times, like the great festivals of Christmas and Easter, we
shall let ourselves go as at a party with all the rich colors,
lovely music, trumpets, dancing, incense, expressions of
joy and affection which will say not in words but in atmosphere, "Christ is born, Christ is risen."

We also need to see worship as the *redeeming of life*.
To this end the life of the week preceding the worship
will be brought into the experience of worship as a
proper focusing of reality. For example, groups can meet
to thresh out the disclosure of epistle and gospel to the
situations they have been facing in the world; sometimes the Word of God can be preached by a layman
expressing both for himself and for the group what God
is disclosing to him about the reality of himself and his
world. Another suggestion is to let the differences within
the congregation not be the subject of hostile groups or
malicious gossip but rather be brought to the surface in
the confession. This could be made by representatives of
groups who feel division—and it would allow them to
spread out before God their own darkness and find
through him their reconciliation. Outside the regular
Eucharist, occasions and types of both Eucharist and other
worship could express common themes of living
through the use of drama, art, music, and discussions.
The test of the validity of Communion is not some external authorization by the church or bishop but the test of
the real togetherness of love and common action. Com-

mon worship is the natural focusing of this found community. In these and many other ways, worship will truly express the redemption of life, and not just say so.

Worship also expresses the *transcendence of life*. "Thy kingdom come on earth" but also "here we have no abiding city." In worship we find the dual emphasis of both the immanence of God and the transcendence of God—the sense of God in the midst of us, but also God as the ultimate reality, the ground of our being, the love which I now only know as in a glass darkly. We need to be reminded in our worship equally of the God found in the factory and the God who is the heart and glory of all creation. If worship becomes too matter-of-fact and ordinary, we may well lose the divine depth of life.

Here then, let us use the arts, where it is realized that truth is as much communicated by images as by words. The language in which we speak of God is likely to be much nearer that of the artist than that of the scientist, for everything we say of God is like a familiar image reaching out to the reality beneath. Music, poetry, architectural beauty, pictures, and sculpture can be worship and prayer, for they are ways by which truth reaches us. Do not let us lose the language of art; we need more than bare bones (the writers of liturgies might remember this). We want what we say about God understandable, but we do not want to lose the splendor of the glory. If we cut out the numinous, we will be losing an important way of expressing the truth of God and of ourselves, as made in his image—and the numinous in worship is best expressed through the use of *silence* and of *beauty* in music, word, and form.

Let then the Prayer of Togetherness in worship express celebration, redemption, and transcendence or, in simpler terms, joy and sorrow, love and justice, glory and wonder. Then worship may not become, as it often is, the expression of the deadness of modern living, but may become the expression and focusing of that abundant life to which we are called by our praying of life.

CHAPTER 8

The Prayer of Finality

Ironically the age in which we live prides itself on its so-called realism, but we seem quite unable to face the realism of old age and death. We lay enormous stress on youth and the apex of a person's success in life comes at a younger and younger age. A friend of mine said to me recently, "In my profession (advertising), one is too old at 40 for any further advancement." Nevertheless, medical advances have enabled people to live longer and longer, so that it is now possible to have reached the peak of our work's endeavors only halfway through our actual life. We can no longer then regard retirement as leaving only a few years of life; it may well be that retirement in the future will come at about fifty, leaving, perhaps, thirty or more years of life before us.

In the same way, we seem incapable of facing death as a fact. In a recent newspaper article on death, the writer said, "Death is as untouchable a subject as was sex in Victorian England." Now we can talk endlessly about sex but never about death. Taboo or not taboo? Is this the "rub" in Britain's national attitude to death? Are the ludicrous trappings of American funeral parlors with the embalming of the body, masses of flowers, music, and so forth, an attempt to cast a facade of unreality even over the reality of death? Do we abolish mourning rituals (twenty minutes for each funeral in our local crematorium and woe betide you with the undertakers if you are a moment longer!) because we wish to avoid the thought of our own mortality? Having become less confident of what lies beyond death, are we less willing than previous generations to confront it? We even do not like using the word; we talk of "passing on" or "passing over." But we do not pass on or pass over; we die. The only certain fact in life is that one day we shall die.

It would be wrong, therefore, to end this book without looking briefly at what prayer as we have understood it will mean in the facing of old age and death.

THE PRAYER OF OLD AGE

The great value of learning quite early in life that the times of disengagement are as important in the rhythm of life as the times of activity is that we shall learn how to lay up a treasure store for old age. Old age is the time when interior activity takes the place of exterior activity. An old age in which the mind is filled with much reading and reflection in the past will never be boring. Not only will there be rich memories but also a storehouse of discovery by which the final decisions of life before death can be faced. Then I shall have built up a life in which both the times of disengagement and engagement have been times of searching for that reality which at last will be more fully disclosed to me by death. Death will be simply the last surrender of a life of daily surrenders and penetrations through the facades to the real. If, on the other hand, our whole life before retirement has been one in which reading, study, and reflection played little part, the spaces of solitude which old age inevitably brings will simply be spaces of boredom and frustration.

Through my attempts to find the reality of myself, I should try to learn in old age that certain surrenders have now become inevitable and may be gracefully made. These range from the surrender of that independence which refuses to let others do things to the surrender of possessions which can no longer be of any real importance to living. One of the saddest things to witness in the lives of some old people is that their clinging to possessions becomes even stronger. It is, I suppose, an indication that the security of the true self rooted in God has not yet been found, and the only security still known when friends and relatives have gone is the security of the things one has accumulated. I know of an old lady of eighty-seven whose house is full of priceless and valuable things and she lives in perpetual fear of burglary. There are many younger people who could benefit from some of these possessions for she has no dependent relatives, but she still will not part with anything. How very different for a true reality of living if she could have had a few years watching some young person helped by the use of her things. Hopefully we can use old age by continuing reflection upon the need to die to find new life. Then perhaps we can learn to make the final surrenders of the material securities which have often blinded us to the true realities of living.

Also, there can be a rich bond between young and old through the capacity in old age to have a contemplative experience of life. The old have the ability to be still and to listen, the time to chat, to tell stories, to play games, to be a little childlike and irresponsible in a way which the young find liberating. The fierce urgency which marks our middle years fades in the old, and we have a new sense of time which makes us more available to people who need time, as many young people do. Often they find their grandparents more sympathetic to their problems than their parents.

THE FACING OF DEATH

There are certain stages in the prayer of facing death, the prayer of finality, which are supremely important to a good death.

First, if I have searched for reality in life, then I do not let my last moments be moments of supreme unreality when everyone is hiding from me the fact that I am dying, and I am colluding with this by trying to hide the fact from myself. There may be controversy about this from the medical point of view, but there can surely be no controversy from the Christian viewpoint. We insult the dignity and responsibility of a human being if we do not allow him, if it is possible, the right to meet such an important enemy as death.

The fear of death is the fear of the unknown. To pray then my death is to be able to enter into those fears and share them with those whom I have loved in life. There is much to be done, much to be shared in those last days of life. The opportunity is there to be closer together in real living than has been possible for years. Even if I am to be terrified by the knowledge of my approaching death, let me have the opportunity to work through that terror with those who will help me, rather than let my last days with the family be days of pretense and deceit. As Christ faced his Gethsemane, may I face my death, the better for facing it in advance in all its terror.

I watched my father die in the full knowledge of his approaching death and with that dignity which enabled us to read the great passages in St. John's gospel about "In my Father's house are many mansions" and discuss their meaning. Then after that reading he spoke individually to each member of the family about life and death, and we received our last Communion together. Since then I have been in no doubt as to whether we should be allowed to know our death. A woman I knew to be dying said to me, "When my sister died, we played the game according to the usual rules; we kept it from her and she died unnecessarily lonely. Now it is my turn and I have brought into the open my knowledge of my coming death. I don't have to watch faces for clues. My family is spared the intolerable burden of pretense, and I can share my fears with my husband."

To pray my death is to know that I shall be lonely and

to accept the constant presence with me of those whom I love. They may not need to say much, but simply to be there in the last hours and to hold my hand or put an arm round me as I am dying will be more important than many words. It is also valuable to allow others to mourn with me so that their grief may not be locked up. This is also very important after death. There is no need to praise the "stiff upper lip," the outwardly unmoved bearing. A psychiatrist writes, "The capacity to mourn the loss of a loved person is a necessity for a human being. If grief is properly worked through, the part of himself which the dead person gave while alive is absorbed into the living person who can then continue the process of healthy living. If the grief is not worked through, this process may be halted."

But, above all, to pray my death is to know that I shall face the last darkness before the completion of union with God. How revealing that the last experience of Christ was utter aloneness even from God, "My God, my God, why hast thou forsaken me?" Then, almost immediately, this was followed by the ultimate union with God, "Father, into thy hands I commend my spirit."

At the moment of death, we face the supreme aloneness of life. Even those whom I loved in life will suddenly become unimportant to me. A sister who has cared for the dying for twenty years said that often at the very end, it was quite clear that although the one dying had wanted their last hours to be with their loved ones, they had no longing to stay with them. Perhaps in that moment we shall know, as did Christ, the most complete dark night of all. Because love for us has meant love found in others and from others, and that love has suddenly become unreal, we may not immediately grasp that it is because we are at last to find what we have been striving for— the pure surrender to God. It may seem for a moment like total loss, but the loss will, I believe, immediately be followed by a climaxing experience of reality in which, at last, all the fullness of eternal life is revealed to us.

I shall, of course, wish to prepare for that last surrender and darkness. Here I shall use the graces which God through his church gives me. I shall want the priest to hear my last confession and receive my last Absolution— that the darknesses within me may finally be penetrated. I shall want to receive the Anointing which is the symbol of wholeness and healing which is just around the corner. I shall want to receive Communion with all who have shared the reality of the bread and wine of life with me and with all who have attempted, however feebly, with me to receive the reality of life in Christ into the bread and wine of living. Then I shall be ready to hear, as I would wish to hear, as the last aloneness closes round me, the great words of Commendation:

> Go forth, O Christian soul, out of the world
> In the name of God the Father who created thee,
> In the name of Jesus Christ who redeemed thee.
> In the name of the Holy Spirit who sanctifieth thee.

If all deaths could have these great preparations for dying, what a restoration of diginity and reality to death there would be!

CONCLUSION

The prayers of finality, the prayers of death, spell out the whole search of this book. The search for reality in life is expressed through reflection, through study of the disclosures of God, through the living out personally and in togetherness a real and full life, but the final end of all spheres of the search is the realization of union with our true selves, which is union with God. That is why prayer is the means to reality. For this reason, the realization of all our prayer living is finally found at death. I will close then with two quotations which eloquently give expression to this.

When the signs of age begin to mark my body (and still more when they touch my mind); when the ill that is to diminish me or carry me off strikes from without or is born within me; when the painful moment comes in which I suddenly awaken to the fact that I am growing ill or growing old; and above all at that last moment when I feel that I am losing hold of myself and am absolutely passive within the hands of the great unknown forces that have formed me; in all these dark moments, O God, grant that I may understand that it is you (provided only my faith is strong enough) who are painfully parting the fibres of my being in order to penetrate to the very marrow of my substance and bear me away within yourself.[1]

Teilhard de Chardin

For in death we are caught up again, invaded, dominated by the divine power. Death surrenders us totally to God; it is there we must at last be united fully with Him. Let us surrender ourselves to death in absolute love, absolute trust, absolute self-abandonment. There is no need to fear. In death there is peace, fulfillment, joy. To die will be a great adventure.[2]

F. C. Happold

One might add, as a final word, that to die will be a great adventure, if to live has been a great adventure; for both life and death will be a "dropping out into God."

ACKNOWLEDGMENTS

CHAPTER 1:   Living and Half-Living

1. John Coburn, *Spirituality for Today* (London: S.C.M. Press, 1967), p. 21.
2. Charles A. Reich, *The Greening of America* (New York: Random House, 1970, copyright © 1970 by Charles A. Reich), p. 9.
3. Nicola Chiaromonte, as quoted in Theodore Roszak, *The Making of a Counter Culture* (Garden City, New York: Doubleday and Company, Inc., 1969), p. 23.
4. Theodore Roszak, *The Making of a Counter Culture* (Garden City, N. Y.: Doubleday and Company, Inc., 1969), p. 15.
5. John A. T. Robinson, *Honest to God* (Philadelphia: The Westminster Press, 1963), p. 91.

CHAPTER 2:   Praying My Life

1. Pierre Teilhard de Chardin, *The Phenomenon of Man* (New York: Harper and Row, Publishers, 1959), p. 165.
2. M. C. D'Arcy, S. J., *Mirage and Truth* (New York: The Macmillan Company, 1935), p. 29.
3. Marie-Magdeleine Davy, *The Mysticism of Simone Weil* (Boston, Massachusetts: The Beacon Press, 1951), pp. 42-43.

CHAPTER 3:   The Prayer of Reflection

1. Antoine de Saint-Exupéry, *Flight to Arras* from compilation entitled *Airman's Odyssey* (New York: Harcourt, Brace and World, Inc., 1967), p. 347.
2. F. C. Happold, *Mysticism: A Study and an Anthology* (Baltimore, Maryland: Penguin Books, Inc., 1970), p. 70. Reprinted by permission of Penguin Books, Ltd.
3. F. C. Happold, *Mysticism,* p. 70.

4. J. M. Déchanet, O.S.B., *Christian Yoga* (London: Search Press Limited, 1960), pp. 83-84.

5. John Burnaby, *Soundings* (Cambridge: Cambridge University Press, 1962), p. 235.

6. Trevor Huddleston, *Naught for Your Comfort* (Garden City, N. Y.: Doubleday and Company, 1956), p. 16.

7. St. John of the Cross, *The Ascent of Mount Carmel* (Westminster, Maryland: The Newman Press, 1949), Book I, Chapter II, verse 1.

8. Frank C. Happold, *Mysticism,* p. 94.

CHAPTER 5:   Praying with the Bible

1. Pierre Teilhard de Chardin, *The Divine Milieu* (New York: Harper and Row, Publishers, Inc., 1960), p. 70.

CHAPTER 6:   The Prayer of the Now

1. John Lehmann, *In My Own Time* (Boston, Massachusetts: Little, Brown and Company, 1969), p. 303.

CHAPTER 7:   The Prayer of Togetherness

1. Charles Reich, *The Greening of America* (New York: Random House, 1970), p. 251.

CHAPTER 8:   The Prayer of Finality

1. Pierre Teilhard de Chardin, *The Divine Milieu (New* York: Harper and Row, Publishers, 1960), pp. 89-90.

2. F. C. Happold, *Prayer and Meditation* (Baltimore, Maryland: Penguin Books, Inc., 1971), p. 355.